Ár nDraíocht Féin: A Druid Fellowship

The ADF Dedicant Path
Through the Wheel of the Year
(Fifth Edition)

A Working Guide

By Rev. Michael J Dangler
(with a lot of help from the Dedicants of ADF)

Created & Compiled by Rev. Michael J Dangler
Cover by Rev. James "Seamus" Dillard
Fifth Edition (2016) (v. 5.0)
r3.2.2016

PDF available for free use by ADF members
In completing the ADF Dedicant Path documentation
And finding their own way along this Path

eBook (.epub/.mobi), physical book,
and accompanying materials available only through:

www.magicaldruid.com

The Magical Druid
3165 N High St.
Columbus, OH 43202

Three Cranes Grove, ADF
www.threecranes.org
Columbus, OH

The ADF Dedicant Path Through the Wheel of the Year

Table of Contents

Introduction: Using this document, tricks and tips, and acknowledgements

A video introduction to this book is available at
http://bit.ly/dp-woty-intro

When I began my Dedicant Path work in 2001, there was no clear plan, with homework, for completing the documentation. Requests for such a path seem to have borne fruit, for one day in 2005 I finally sat down to write the document you now see.

It's important to note that the completion of the Dedicant Path documentation is *not* a primary focus of the DP. The Dedicant Path is about walking your walk, and learning to walk at your own pace and in your own way. We hope to show all our Dedicants not only how to write a book report, but also how to walk the Path that is in their heart. Indeed, if our Dedicants never write a book report, but they know how to walk the Path they wish to walk, then we have succeeded in our aims.

That said, the documentation and the Path are not exclusive to one another. Since its first edition, this book has been about using the requirements in the DP documentation to help the Path *emerge* for the seeker who needs structure and discipline in order to find their way. Each lesson is like a signpost, a blaze on a tree, or an arrow chalked onto a rock. The lessons mark paths you can take: paths full of knowledge, experimentation, and lore. Please feel free to take a wander in any direction these symbols may point you!

This Fifth Edition represents a change from previous editions by drawing in some additional work, adding in more structure, including meditations, to help direct the student's work. **This book, as it has always been, is not an official guide to the DP, but rather one way of working through it.** You will do more work than is required by the bare documentation requirements if you work this plan, and I hope that this will help you find greater depth to your spirituality.

This book is far more in-depth than the requirements for the documentation are. The most obvious example is the First Oath, which is not a requirement but which has value beyond the listed requirements and builds a spiritual background to draw from. At times, this book also takes a more difficult approach where there are options, such as in the case of the meditation journal. That requirement does not require an essay, but this book treats the essay option as the better of the two, so that the student may learn more and forge a deeper understanding of herself in the process of remembering and reflecting on the options.

Previous versions of this book had some difficulty with scheduling High Days. Primarily, the High Days fall an average of 6.5 weeks apart, so you will occasionally run into times when the High Day comes a bit late or a tad early for the lesson.

A trick that I've come across for making this work is that when you come to a High Day rite preparation or re-cap before your calendar calls for it, take a week off. It may cost you some time, but it's a good (and common) solution.

Another option, of course, is to double up assignments on the week a High Day falls. That is often less attractive, but it's certainly doable. A week is more than enough time to do any of the homework listed. In fact, most of the homework should take about two to three hours of writing, total (mediation or ritual time not included).

Also, you don't have to wait for two weeks before the next High Day to start walking the Path. If a High Day is coming up fast, the first two weeks can be compressed. If it's a few weeks away, they can be stretched out. If you're looking to stretch out the weeks, I'd suggest taking a couple of weeks to get to know the DP Handbook, *Our Own Druidry*, by reading through it, and also getting acquainted with the ADF Members' site. Both these tools will be very valuable to walking this Path.

Thanks in particular go out to Jenni, who set the current standards so clearly; Raven, who helped me re-work this book; Ian, who wrote *Our Own Druidry* and gave several pointers that helped me figure out how to adapt it; Narabali for getting *Oak Leaves* back on track, and for encouraging and adding DP-related articles back into that publication; Vedis and more recent ADF Chroniclers for continuing to hold *Oak Leaves* to that standard; the LiveJournal community that actually got me writing these homeworks; the DP mentors for asking for such a document (and reviewing it when it was ready); Jessie for creating and letting me sub in on a class built from this book; Cei for his wonderful prayers; and Linda for inspiring me to do the final push to get this edited.

Thanks also to all those who write the articles and books, give the workshops at festivals, and support the Dedicants in all their efforts; and thanks to the Dedicants who teach me every day.

Special thanks are offered to Three Cranes Grove, ADF, members Misty, Nick, and Anna for running through this training manual with me, and being my test subjects. They've shown me several of the issues directly related to this document, and have been instrumental in getting them fixed.

It has been a true joy to write this book, and to hear from the many people who have enjoyed and profited from the information within. Thank you for using the book, and thank you for walking this Path with ADF, with our Groves and Protogroves, with our Solitaries, and with me!

-Rev. Michael J Dangler
Grove Priest
Three Cranes Grove, ADF
Columbus, OH

Week 1: Personal Religion and an Introduction

Related to Requirement: Not related to a specific requirement.
Required Reading:
- *Our Own Druidry*, p. 11-18 (Introduction)
- *Our Own Druidry*, p. xi - xii (Appendix B: "Required Documentation")
- *DP FAQ*: <http://www.adf.org/members/training/dp/faq.html>

Suggested Reading:
- "Journaling the Druid Path" by Ladytoad
  <http://www.adf.org/members/training/dp/articles/journaling-the-druid-path.html>
- "Uncertainty and the Dedicants' Journey" by Arthur Shipkowski,
  <https://www.adf.org/training/dedicant/uncertainty.html>

Brightest Blessings, and welcome to the first step on the journey that is the ADF Dedicant Path! The required reading for this lesson is mostly to give you a feel for what to expect over the next year.

First Things First: What's a Dedicant?
This is a bit of a strange thing within ADF, because it has some different meanings when we look at the word. If you are journaling online or with a word processor, you may notice that "Dedicant" is not a word recognized by most standard dictionaries. That's okay: sometimes, we Druids enjoy tweaking the system a bit.

In ADF, a Dedicant is someone who has decided to walk the path of Druidry. Many people will use the term "Dedicant" to describe themselves when they begin walking the path, and it is just fine for you to call yourself an "ADF Dedicant" right now: the fact that you're involved in training shows dedication, after all.

The term was originally meant to describe those who have completed the documentation of the ADF Dedicant Path, but these days we mostly refer to those individuals as "Dedicated Druids," rather than as "Dedicants," mostly because of the folk process that's started calling everyone a Dedicant.

In the end, there's hardly a right or wrong way to define what a "Dedicant" is in ADF, except that one who is a "Dedicant" is actively engaged in study and in the process of self-improvement that comes with being dedicated to that study.

Supplies You May Need:
In order to go through the course of study we'll be presenting you with, you will find certain things very useful. To that end, we've made you a sort of "school supply" list that will hopefully help you:

- ***Our Own Druidry***: This document, also known as the "Dedicant Handbook" or the "Dedicant Manual" is the most basic reference text you will need in order to get started. Of course, we recommend reading it all the way through, but most lessons will have some reading from this book that focuses on the lesson. This is received in your Membership Packet when you join ADF, and is also available in electronic format on the ADF site. You can obtain it in print through Amazon or The Magical Druid.

- **Dedicant Notebook:** In this, you will record some basic things, such as journal entries, impressions, notes from your reading, etc. It is often best to keep it electronically, but a paper journal is also acceptable. Whatever you do, though, back this up! Notebooks in computer form have been lost to power failure, burned-out hard drives, and degaussed disks. Notebooks in paper form have been lost to house fires, pets with a taste for knowledge, and even enemy fire in Iraq. No, we're not joking. CD backups and trips to the local copy machine will save you *months* of work if something happens to your original. If you are interested in a paper journal that matches this book, you can find it on Amazon, or at The Magical Druid.

  If you choose to record your work online, you can use the hashtag **#dpwoty** to help connect with other Dedicants. There's a list of blogs and resources at the end of this introduction.

- **Meditation Journal:** This can be the same as your Dedicant Notebook, but some people prefer to keep them separate. The same caveats go for this as go for the notebook, though: *make a backup!*

- **An e-mail program, or access to e-mail:** Email is the best way to get quick answers from other Dedicants or your mentor. You can subscribe to many ADF lists here, or visit the forums: <http://www.adf.org/members/forums/subscribe.html>, and you should most certainly be subscribed to the main email list: **ADF-Dedicants**.

- **Access to the ADF website:** Not only can the DP document be accessed from there, but you can find all the back issues of *Oak Leaves* and *Druid's Progress* on the site as well at <http://www.adf.org/members/publications/>

- **A subscription to *Oak Leaves*:** It's always good to have the issues in hand, just in case. Start collecting now, because they're invaluable tools! You can subscribe using the ADF membership form at <http://www.adf.org/joining/join.html>

- **Some way to write your final essays:** This should be different from your Dedicant Notebook, because you'll be keeping things in the Notebook that might be very personal, or that aren't required for the Dedicant Path at all. Type the final essays on a computer so that you can submit electronically. And again: ***Make regular backups!***

- **A calendar or planner:** It may sound silly, but a calendar to keep track of what is due when can be remarkably helpful, and you might want to sit down and plot out when certain major events, like High Days, book report completion targets, and your Dedicant Oath rite are set for. It will also certainly help to plan out a two to three hour block of time each week for DP work. And if you put it into your planner or on your calendar, you're less likely to forget. (All "final essays" are marked as such in the table of contents, so you can figure out when things would be "due" with greater ease.)

- **Your library card:** Many ADF members are put off by the cost of purchasing books for the DP and later Study Programs. If you don't have a library card, *go get one* and make close friends with your local librarian!

Also included is a book and resource list. You will work mostly from the *Dedicant Handbook*, but there is supplemental reading that you might find useful when trying to do things or understand them. Don't feel like you need to go out and purchase them now, or that you absolutely must read them all: they are only offered as suggestions. You'll find a full list of resources (including when they will match the lesson) at the end of this first lesson so that you can plan ahead.

The method of teaching here is very Socratic. In essence, this document will pose questions that will hopefully help you sort out your feelings on your own. The document will not be providing you with answers, but with paths to achieve those answers. You may always feel free to question us back via ADF-Dedicants or a mentor, but even if we wanted to give you the answers, we couldn't: they need to come from your own heart.

Finally, there is also homework. I know, you thought you were done with that when you finished school, right? Each week will not necessarily include homework, but most will. If you do the homework each week, you won't have to write up anything at the end, because it will all be done (and your mentor, if you have one, will be able to give you pointers if it doesn't appear "up to snuff").

A word on mentors: Not everyone wants a mentor, and we don't automatically assign them. If you want one, you need to contact the ADF Preceptor, or else the deputy in charge of mentoring. If you have any questions, please contact the person in charge of mentoring at <ADF-Mentor-Request@adf.org> for information about mentoring. They will forward your information onto an available mentor, who should answer you. This process of matching mentor to mentee can take some time, so please be patient after requesting.

Instead of a mentor, you might also consider working with another person on your Dedicant Path, either using this document or working in a more free-form way. On the ADF Wiki, a page has been set up where you can link up with other Dedicants looking for a partner as well. You can either search the ADF website for "Dedicant Buddies" or you can go directly to <https://www.adf.org/members/wiki/dedicantbuddies/index.html>.

Now, let's move on and get you started on your DP, shall we? We'll start small, and begin to work our way up.

Homework:

Some questions may be raised by the introduction and the requirements, and that is good, for we very much wish all of our Dedicants to go into this path with open minds, open hearts, and open eyes. Some questions that might come up you will certainly need to answer, and your assignment for the next week is to consider these questions carefully.

- Why have you chosen to take the first steps on the Dedicant Path?
- Is this a step on your path, or will this become the Path itself?
- What do you expect to learn?
- What would you like to get out of this journey?
- Do you know where this path will take you?
- If you have just joined ADF, why have you chosen to work on this immediately?
- If you have been in ADF for a long time, why are you starting only now?
- Does it look hard or easy?
- Which requirements appear to be difficult to you now, and which appear to be easy?
- Do you have doubts, questions, or concerns that you need to ask about?

Consider each question carefully. Set aside some time before next week and let each question roll around in your mind for a while. The answers to these questions will help light your way when the path becomes dark and difficult, and they will help keep you going through those tough times.

Write your answers in your Dedicant Notebook We will return to them from time to time through the next year.

Brightest blessings to you on this Path, and please let us or your mentor know if you need any help during the week, or have any questions!

Additional resources mentioned throughout the course:

Things Mentioned Throughout:

- ***Our Own Druidry***, referred to in this work sometimes as the *Dedicant Handbook* or *Dedicant Manual*
- ***Oak Leaves, Druid's Progress***, various issues. Nearly all articles referenced in this work are available on the ADF website, and web addresses will be given for specific articles.
- **The ADF Website** (access to the Members' side is required for access to all the information and articles listed and is included in your ADF membership)

- **The Three Cranes Grove, ADF, website**, which offers several useful pages, but particularly useful is http://www.threecranes.org/meditations. This page includes a large body of guided meditations that are of great use for an ADF Dedicant, including several you'll run into in this book, and we're expanding that page all the time. Some are recorded in ritual, and some are recorded without background noise. As the home Grove for the author, we've worked hard to make sure that this page really provides a lot of resources.

General Resource Items by Week:

Week 2:
- Ceisiwr Serith's A Book of Pagan Prayer (ISBN: 1578632552)

Week 3:
- Rev. Michael J Dangler's *Crane Breviary and Guide Book*, available in preview (including everything you'll need for your Dedicant work in this book) on the ADF site: <https://www.adf.org/system/files/members/orders/crane/print/cbgb-preview.pdf>, or available in full via <http://magicaldruid.com/shop/>
- Three Cranes Grove, ADF's, *The Fire on Our Hearth – A Three Cranes Devotional*, available through <http://magicaldruid.com/shop/> (ISBN: 0615879799)
- Rev. Skip Ellison's *The Solitary Druid*, ISBN: 0806526750
- Nicholas Egelhoff's *Sunna's Journey: Norse Liturgy Through the Wheel of the Year*, ISBN 978-0615880242

Week 6:
- A Recommended Reading List, <http://www.adf.org/training/resources/recommended.html>

Week 7:
- Ian Corrigan, *Sacred Fire, Holy Well* (ISBN: 0976568128)

Week 8:
- Ian Corrigan's CD, "Training the Mind: Techniques of Trance and Meditation," available at <https://tredara.bandcamp.com/album/training-the-mind-a-workshop-in-trance-energy-work-meditation>
- Audio Meditations at the Three Cranes Grove, ADF, website: <http://threecranes.org/meditations/>
- DP WotY specific audio meditations at the Three Cranes Grove, ADF, website: <http://threecranes.org/meditations/dpwoty/>

Week 11:
- Two Powers Audio file: <https://www.adf.org/system/files/members/training/dp/twopowers.mp3>;

Week 12:
- *An Awfully Big Adventure: Signposts on the Soul's Journey Through the Indo-European Afterlife* by Rev. Michael J Dangler <https://www.youtube.com/watch?v=Szqz9Clyfa0>

Week 13:

- <u>A Virtuous Life</u> Nine Virtues study guide:
  <<https://www.adf.org/system/files/members/training/dp/publications/dp-req-1-nine-virtues.pdf>>

Week 19:

- Rev. Michael J Dangler's Dedicant Oath,
  <<http://www.chronarchy.com/mjournal/oath/>>

Week 24:

- Ian Corrigan, "Working Magic with the Two Powers"
  <<https://www.adf.org/articles/working/two-powers-magic.html>>

Week 33

- *The Man Who Planted Trees* by Jean Giono (ISBN: 1570625387; text available at <<http://home.infomaniak.ch/arboretum/Man_Tree.htm>>)

Week 44:

- *Real Magick* by Isaac Bonewits (1989 edition, ISBN: 0877286884)

Social Media Resources

When it comes to online resources, there are a lot out there. You can connect with people via Facebook, YouTube, Twitter, Instagram, Tumblr, or any number of other social media services (even Snapchat). As mentioned above, there's a universal hashtag you can use to connect (new to the 5th Edition of this work, so it might take some time to build if you're reading this in 2016): **#dpwoty**.

Before the release of this document, a group of ADF Priests started creating items that would supplement the DP work found in this manual online. On most services, you'll find *something* on the #dpwoty hashtag, but if there isn't anything, then I encourage you to create it. Hashtags can't be moderated or controlled, but I'm hopeful that it can be at least unique enough to help people connect without a lot of other noise.

If you are looking for more established places to learn and grow, I recommend the following places:

- **#dpwoty** and **#adfdruidry** are the two best hashtags to search for things related to the path of Druidry, as practiced here and within ADF. I hope you will create your own content on those tags, as well.
- The official ADF Dedicants forum on the ADF website (mentioned above; the only truly official space for Dedicants in ADF). Subscribe at http://www.adf.org/members/forums/subscribe.html
- <u>**The ADF Druidry official social media accounts:**</u>
  - Official ADF Facebook page: <https://www.facebook.com/adfdruidry>
  - Official ADF Facebook discussion: https://www.facebook.com/groups/323869237675238/

- Official ADF Facebook Solitaries community: https://www.facebook.com/groups/317663451579022/
- Official ADF Twitter account: https://twitter.com/adfdruidry
- Official ADF YouTube account: https://www.youtube.com/user/adfutube
- Official ADF MySpace account: https://myspace.com/adfdruidry
- Official ADF G+ account: https://plus.google.com/+ArnDraoichtFeinADFADruidFellowshipInc/posts
- IRC Chatroom: https://www.adf.org/forums/chats/irc/mibbit.html

- **Unofficial ADF Druidry social media accounts:**
  - ADF Druidry on Tumblr: http://adfdruidry.tumblr.com/
  - Dedicants of Indo-European Paganism: https://www.facebook.com/groups/ie.dedicants/
  - The ADF Dedicant LiveJournal community: if you have an LJ or want to blog but not manage the platform, this might be a good option (though it's not as active as it once was: it's over 10 years old as of this writing, and is the second oldest of our social media accounts). Find it at: http://dedicants.livejournal.com/profile
  - The ADF LiveJournal community: This is the oldest of ADF's active social media accounts. http://adf.livejournal.com/profile

- **Other useful social media links**
  - The Three Cranes Grove, ADF, YouTube account: https://www.youtube.com/3CGVideos
  - Rev. Kirk Thomas (Archdruid as of this writing) on YouTube: https://www.youtube.com/user/druidkirk
  - The Magical Druid YouTube account: https://www.youtube.com/user/MagicalDruid

- **The Author:** If you're interested in finding me on social media sites, you can almost always find my information under the username "chronarchy," or else my full name, "Michael J Dangler." I always welcome feedback on this book and love to chat with Dedicants: please don't be embarrassed to add me randomly to whatever social media site you find me on.

  My own Dedicant Path work is available at my website, Chronarchy.Com, specifically at: http://www.chronarchy.com/mjournal. I encourage you to reach out to other ADF Priests and members as well for support on the journey: virtually everyone loves to help our Dedicants.

Week 2: The First Oath

Related to Requirement: Not related to a specific requirement

Required Reading:

- *Our Own Druidry*, p. 16-17 (The First Oath)
- "Chanting the First Oath Everyday" by Brandon:
  <http://www.adf.org/members/training/dp/articles/first-oath-chant.html>

Recommended Reading:

- Ceisiwr Serith's A Book of Pagan Prayer p.8 – 12 ("Why Do We Make Offerings?" and "The 'Politics' of Giving")

Now that you know the answers to some basic questions, or at least have an idea of them, we will move onto the First Oath.

Isn't it a little soon for an oath? Not at all. The First Oath is not an oath before others, or an oath to ADF, the Archdruid, a specific deity, or even your mentor. It is an oath that is between you, the deities, and the spirits. You may choose whether to do this oath in public or in private, but it should be done on or before the next High Day Rite.

Most importantly, the First Oath is not at all required for the Dedicant Path Documentation. It's added in for those who wish to commit to study on this path in a formal way. This oath is *not* your Dedicant Oath (we'll do that at the end of this book).

If you know your patron deities already, or the hearth culture you will be working in, you may make an oath to those deities, but for the majority of Dedicants, the deities and powers they will eventually worship, honor, or follow are still unknown, standing in the shadows of our consciousness, guiding us with unseen hands. Because of this, the First Oath is not designed to be given to a specific deity or group of deities.

There is an example First Oath on pages 16 – 17 of *Our Own Druidry*. As you prepare to take your First Oath, refer to this example. Does it say the words you want said? Are there parts that are uncomfortable? Are there parts you could have written if you were speaking from your own heart? If you wish, you can use the exact wording of the oath on this page, or you can take the general idea and replace the words.

Please, do not state in this oath that you will finish your Dedicant Path, especially not within a certain amount of time. If you make that oath and decide not to finish it, or that ADF is not for you, you will need to answer to the powers you oathed to.

Think of ways to make your oath that fit your personality and skills: re-work the example into a song that you can sing; add an offering of silver to a local river to seal the bargain; take the words and turn them into dance steps and make your oath in that way. Be creative, but be sure to stay mindful of the intent of this First Oath.

This is a binding oath, and when you make it, you are swearing to these deities that you will lead a virtuous, pious, studious life, and that you will worship them and honor them to the best of your ability.

An oath should be contained in a ritual. Because many are new to this path, we have written a simple self-blessing ritual that you can use for this oath. Please make sure that you read it all the way through before performing it: it is good practice to always know what comes next in a ritual you have committed to doing. This ritual has an option for offerings, but none are explicitly required in order to work this first ritual. The aim of the ritual is to seek blessings and make that First Oath.

A note on making offerings: Often, you will hear or read about offerings of silver to the well, offerings of food or drink to the Ancestors, or offerings of oil to the Deities. Silver is a common offering in most rituals[1] and is often given to the well or put into running water. The best place to find offerings of silver is a local fabric or bead store, where small silver beads can be found for less than a dollar each. The "oil" referred to is generally olive oil or another good cooking oil from a native European plant, and the oil is often poured onto an open (and outdoor) flame. As to why we make this sort of offering? Check out Ceisiwr Serith's *A Book of Pagan Prayer*, the sections titled "Why Do We Make Offerings?" and "The 'Politics' of Giving" for an excellent summation of the reasons.

---

[1] Silver is often *not* offered in Vedic ritual, because Vedic texts refer to it as the "tears of Agni (fire)," so offering silver to the Vedic gods is like offering sorrow to them. "The tear that was shed became silver; therefore silver is not a suitable gift, for it is born of tears" (Yajurveda I.V.1, *The Rekindling of the Fire*")

A Simple Self Blessing and First Oathing

Set up a working altar: it should include a candle, a vessel of water, and a representation of a tree. Relax, and begin.

Take a moment to focus on your breathing. As you breathe in, feel the breath fill your lungs, and as you breathe out, feel it expel completely. Concentrate on this for a three or four breaths, and then turn your attention to the earth. Feel the earth below you, the firm ground. Experience the earth as upholding you, as maintaining your weight. Feel the earth holding you, rather than you pushing against the earth.

Earth Mother, I stand upon you today and recognize that we begin with you and we will end with you. Uphold me now as I give praise, and support me as I receive blessing.

A child of the earth, I come before the Gods, the Spirits of Nature, and the Ancestors to offer praise. I seek to establish ties, to offer to them and open to them in return.

The waters support and surround me.
The land extends about me.
The sky stretches out above me.
At the center burns a living flame.[2]

I call out to the Keeper of the Gates.
Though I walk on uncertain paths,
Though I travel on unmapped ground,
Guide me, ward me, and relay my voice
As I offer prayers and praise.

In your mind's eye, see the sacred center open before you: watch the mists part, see the door to the Otherworld open, or watch the spiral of the magic from between the worlds reveal the Otherworld. The Gates are now open, and the true work can begin.

I call out to my ancestors, those who came before me, you of my blood and you of my heart. I seek to give you praise, to remember you now, and to honor you.

Think on your ancestors: see their faces, smile with joy at their presence. If you have praise to give them, do so now.

I call out to the spirits of this place, the spirits of nature who are the soul of this land. I seek to give you praise, to call out to you now, and to honor you.

---

[2] Serith, 36. As you speak these words, visualize the world as described here: the waters support the land, and the sky stretches out above us. This living flame burns at the center, and at the center of each of us.

Think on the nature spirits: the faeries of the wood, the spirits of the land. If you have praise to give them, do so now.

I call out to the deities, first children, eldest and wisest. It is you to whom we look for guidance, and you who grant the greatest blessings. I seek to give you praise, to honor you now, to give you due worship.

Think on the deities: the great ones who bless our lives, who watch over us and show us that unconditional love. If you have praise to give them, do so now.

[optional] - If you have a patron deity, one that you might wish to offer to specifically, now is the time to do that. If not, simply move to the next portion.

Today, I have given of my praise and myself.
With love in my heart and devotion on my tongue
I call out now, with all my soul:
Accept my praises!

Take a moment to visualize, as you shout this last statement, all of your blessings, praise, and intent flowing up to the gods, out to the spirits of nature, and down to the ancestors. Hold yourself in that moment, watching your praises flow from you, and prepare yourself for what may be offered in return.

Now, take your divination tool up.

As I have given praise to the Powers, I open to them. If there are blessings to be had, what might the nature of those blessings be?

Draw three symbols: one for the Ancestors, one for the Nature Spirits, and one for the Deities. Examine each one, think about the omen offered, and consider how it might translate into blessings.

Now, take these omens and concentrate on them, holding forth a cup of water or other beverage, saying:

Indeed, the Powers offer me blessings. Now I seek the manifestation of those blessings, the outpouring from the Powers that offer them. To those who enter this exchange, pour forth your blessings into my cup!

Envision the blessings before you, either as a mist, or a vortex of energy, or as pictographic representations of individual blessings. Watch them pour into the cup, mixing and infusing with the liquid already inside.

This in my hands is a holy cup of magic, the great blessings offered to me as joyful return of my praises to the Kindreds. Here are the deep waters that flow within the earth and that rain from the sky. These are the waters of life!

I accept this blessing, and I drink it with love and knowledge of the Powers!

(drink)

Filled with the blessings of the Kindreds, I now call out to the powers here gathered to hear me as I give my First Oath as a traveler upon the Dedicant Path in ADF. Hear my words as they arise on the fire, and hear my voice as it resounds in the well!

[speak your oath here]

Now, with joy in my heart, I give thanks: To the Deities, thank you for your blessings. To the Nature Spirits, thank you for your blessings. To the Ancestors, thank you for your blessings. To all those Powers who have aided me, thank you for your blessings.

[If you made an offering to a patron above, make sure you thank him or her first: thank in the reverse order from invitation.]

To the Keeper of the Gates
For guiding me and warding me
Thank you for your protection.

In your mind's eye, see the sacred center close before you: watch the mists gather, see the door to the Otherworld close, or watch the spiral of the magic from between the worlds close in on the Otherworld. The Gates are now closed, and this rite is ending.

Mother of all, to you I will return all things I have left unused. For supporting and upholding me in this rite, I thank you!
This rite is ended!

When you have finished, you should take all your unused offerings and empty them out, and remember that cleaning the altar and space is as important as setting it up.

Homework:

Write your First Oath down in your Dedicant Notebook. You will not be required to turn it in with the rest of your Dedicant materials, but you will find it very useful when you review your progress from time to time, and it will keep you focused on the Dedicant's path when it seems like nothing else will.

One Dedicant, Brandon, found it very useful to recite his First Oath each morning as part of his morning routine. The recitation eventually became chanting, and after a month he noticed that he began to look at that oath from different perspectives. As the chanting went on, the meaning became deeper and more open to him. You can read his experience in his own words here:

<http://www.adf.org/members/training/dp/articles/first-oath-chant.html>

You might try something like what Brandon did, and see if it helps you to more fully internalize the words and meaning of the oath, though this is not required.

Week 3: The first High Holy Day: an explanation

Related to Requirement: #2 – Meaning and Discussion of High Days
Required Reading:

- *Our Own Druidry*, p. 60 – 72 (Hearth Cultures & High Days)
- *ADF Constitution*, Article 4
- *The ADF Core Order of Ritual for High Days*,
  <http://www.adf.org/rituals/explanations/core-order.html>

Optional Reading:

- *Our Own Druidry*, p. 49 – 73 (The Very Basics of Ritual);
- *Appendix 1: Resources and Rituals for the Wheel of the Year* in this book;
- Step by Step through a Druid Worship Ceremony,
  <http://www.adf.org/rituals/explanations/stepbystep.html>;
- The "Liturgy and Rituals" section of the ADF page,
  <http://www.adf.org/rituals/>
- The Three Cranes Grove, ADF, outline of ritual (with example prayers),
  <http://www.threecranes.org/liturgy/>
- *The Crane Breviary and Guide Book* from the Order of the Crane:
  <https://www.adf.org/system/files/members/orders/crane/print/cbgb-preview.pdf>
- Rev. Skip Ellison's *The Solitary Druid*, appropriate high day in Chapters 6 & 7
- Nicholas Egelhoff's *Sunna's Journey: Norse Liturgy Through the Wheel of the Year*, appropriate High Day description

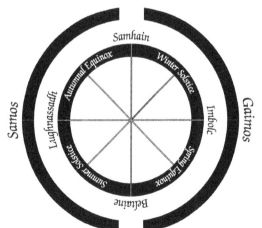

Because this High Holy Day is your first as an ADF Dedicant, this lesson will be longer than the other seven. The same will go for next week's lesson, which will be a recap of the rite you do for this holiday. In this lesson we will talk a bit about why ADF celebrates the 8 Neo-Pagan High Holy Days, what to do if your chosen hearth culture does not celebrate a specific Day, and talk a bit about the urban vs. agrarian worldviews.

ADF celebrates the eight Neo-Pagan High Holy Days. They are celebrated in ADF because we are a Neo-Pagan organization. Not every Indo-European culture celebrated these festivals at the times that ADF and the wider Neo-Pagan community celebrates them, but as we are modern Neo-Pagans (not ancient pagans or reconstructionists), part of our identity relies on the fact that we keep these days holy.

The ADF Constitution outlines the dates of the holidays in Article 4:

Article 4: Calendar

1. *The High Days of the ADF calendar are the eight Neopagan High Days which are the solstices, equinoxes, and points equally between them. For legal purposes, these High Days occur on:*
    a. *Cross-Quarter = November 1st*
    b. *Solstice = December 21st*
    c. *Cross-Quarter = February 1st*
    d. *Equinox = March 21st*
    e. *Cross-Quarter = May 1st*
    f. *Solstice = June 21st*
    g. *Cross-Quarter = August 1st*
    h. *Equinox = September 21st*
2. *For ceremonial purposes, local congregations shall celebrate each of the eight High Days within one week prior to or after the aforementioned dates, or at some other time determined by Board-established policy.*

As you can tell, ADF is very generic about the names and dates, reflecting our IE heritage. The eight High Days are outlined on pages 60 – 72 of *Our Own Druidry*. They are broken down by hearth culture, so that there is information on most of the cultures you might be interested in. Take the description and work to find a compatible feast in your hearth culture for that particular High Day. Remember, too, that you do not need to do the same hearth culture for all of your rituals through your time as an ADF Dedicant: you can always change if something doesn't fit right.

A lot of the High Holy Days are obviously agrarian-based. This can cause some question to come up regarding their relevance. Remember, though, that the great majority of Pagans themselves lived in cities (Rome is an excellent example). Can you find the rhythms of nature in the city? Look hard for them, and I'll bet you can find something fresh and new in your climate that corresponds with this season.

When it comes time to write the ritual, you will need to refer back to the Core Order of Ritual (COoR). To that end, we have included the generic COoR here for your use. The Core Order is designed to be fleshed out by the individual doing the work, which may sound a bit daunting. Additionally, the First Oath ritual you did in Week 2 was a full Core Order of Ritual, so you can take that ritual and modify it to create a High Day ritual by adding a purpose statement about this High Day and honoring a deity specific to this High Day in the Key Offerings section.

Your mentor, of course is available for some help, but we urge you to seek out one of the culture-specific email lists to ask questions on. Quite often, they will be of more help than your mentor can be.

The Core Order of ADF Ritual for High Days

1. Initiating the Rite – *May include*:
   - Musical Signal
   - Opening Prayer
   - Processional
   - Establishing the Group Mind
2. Purification - This must take place prior to Opening the Gates
3. Honoring the Earth Mother
4. Statement of Purpose
5. (Re)Creating the Cosmos
   - Sacred Center must be established in a triadic Cosmos
   - The Three Worlds or Realms must be acknowledged
   - The Fire must be included
   - Sacred Center is most commonly represented as Fire, Well and Tree
6. Opening the Gate(s) - Must include a Gatekeeper
7. Inviting the Three Kindreds
8. Key Offerings - *This will commonly include*:
   - Invitation of Beings of the Occasion
   - Seasonal customs as appropriate
   - Praise Offerings
9. Prayer of Sacrifice
10. Omen
11. Calling (asking) for the Blessings
12. Hallowing the Blessing
13. Affirmation of the Blessing
14. Workings (if any)
15. Thanking the Beings
16. Closing the Gate(s)
17. Thanking the Earth Mother
18. Closing the Rite

Items that ADF Rituals *Do Not* Include

1. Elemental Cross Symbolism (the 4 Elements)
2. Casting Circles in public ritual
3. Calling Watchtowers or Elemental Guardians
4. Calling the dualtheistic "Lord" and "Lady"
5. Acknowledgement of one divine being with power over all
6. Blood Sacrifices
7. Non-Indo-European mythic and deity motifs

Homework:

Now, in your Dedicant Notebook, reflect on this High Holy Day. Consider how it is celebrated in your hearth culture, or across hearth cultures. Are there any myths that are celebrated in connection with this feast? If so, what are they, and how do they fit in? What does this holiday or time of year mean to you? Do you look forward to it? Are there secular aspects of the holiday that mean a lot to you, or perhaps holdovers or memories of your childhood that you cherish? How do you know when this day arrives? Do you look at the calendar, or do you just *know* it has come? If you have children (or wish to have children), what key traditions do you wish to pass down to them? What, if anything, is spiritual or religious to you about this High Day or time of year, and how do you show that? Are there any traditions that your Grove has for this High Day? Finally, is there anything else about this holiday that you would like to add?

There, you've just written your first essay on a High Holy Day, and you're only three weeks into your training! You'll find that all of these essays go similarly.

If you have a local Grove that you attend, then you should already have a rite you can attend. If you are solitary (and even if you do have a Grove, I still recommend), though, you will need to write and perform your own ritual for this rite. Because only four High Days are required to be done as ADF rituals, you don't need to be too concerned with exactly how to do an ADF rite, but you should certainly have something written up, or else go to the ADF website and find a ritual that will fit your hearth culture and use that. Neither your reviewer nor the Kindreds will expect you to be a skilled liturgist this early in the journey. Make sure that you have a rite ready before you intend to do the ritual, though, because last minute ritual writing is never fun for anyone.

See *Appendix 1* for more information on what the High Day is about, where we have provided a number of links to help you think about the High Days themselves (and included places to find some example rituals for you to work from)!

Week 4: First High Day recap

Related to Requirement: #8 – High Days Attended
Required Reading: None.

By now you've made it through your first ritual! Congratulations! It's now time to start your essays for the Dedicant Path documentation by writing a recap of this first High Day rite!

First, we've provided a sort of ritual write-up template that will help you get all the commonly needed details down in Appendix 2. You cannot just turn in a number of those sheets and expect to pass this requirement, though: you need to be much more in-depth. So grab some paper and start thinking about the rite by asking some good questions.

Homework:

Let's start out with an easy one: how did the rite go in terms of structure? What things went wrong during the ritual? What things went right? Who were the patrons of the rite, and who was the gatekeeper? Did you have problems with saying the words without stumbling, or did everything come out smoothly? Did you forget to bring a sacrifice? Were you alone, or with a group? If you were with a group, did you say anything or do anything? Now, for the not so easy part: how did the rite go in terms of function and feeling? Did you feel anything during the ritual? Did you experience doubt or confidence? Can you describe what happened? If you were with a group, what did the other people say about what happened? What omens were drawn (if any), and what did they tell you? Could you feel the presence of any deities, spirits, or powers? What else about the rite struck you, or do you want to share?

If you answer those questions, you've just finished another essay along the Dedicant Path!

Week 5: Nature Awareness 1

Related to Requirement: #7 – Nature Awareness
Required Reading:

- *Our Own Druidry*, p. 39 - 43 (Attunement to Nature & the Kindred)

Optional Reading:

- "Urban Druid" by Mary Jones, <http://www.adf.org/articles/identity/urban-druid.html>;
- "Honoring the Environment Through Religion" by Sylvan, <http://www.adf.org/articles/nature/honoring-the-environment.html>;
- "Loving Our Mother" by Marae Price, <http://www.adf.org/articles/nature/loving-our-mother.html>;
- "Learning from the Trees" by Judith Anderson Morris (Ladytoad), <http://www.adf.org/articles/nature/learning-from-the-trees.html>;

Druidry in general, and ADF Druidry in particular, is not only about scholarship, ritual, and magic; it is also about connecting with the land and the Earth Mother that birthed us and surrounds us. Druidry cannot be divorced from Nature, nor should it be. Our liturgies and oaths describe us as "Children of the Earth", and that is truly what we are.

Whether there an earth mother exists in your primary culture or not, the Earth Mother is a Neo-Pagan goddess who has become central to the workings of ADF over the past thirty years. We call out to her in every ritual, and she upholds us in ritual as she does in our daily lives.

Nature awareness has three facets: the awareness of nature as it exists around us physically; the awareness of the spirits of nature and their relation to us; and the awareness of the Earth Mother herself, and the other deities who are also her children, and the relation of these beings to ourselves. This week, we will examine the nature that exists around us.

It is simple to say that we do not exist apart from nature; it is harder to see this in our everyday lives. Each day, we wake up, shower, put on clothes, eat, and walk out the door to our jobs or school. On cold mornings, the weather is an inconvenience until we get to our destination, and then we spend our whole day working and stressing over details. On hot days we hide in air-conditioned buildings, hoping that our electric bills will remain reasonable. When we return at night, we put dinner in a microwave and watch the nightly news. Where do we have time for nature? Where is it in our lives?

Those of us who live in cities may think we never see nature. We might find ourselves lost in a sea of steel and glass; but even here, nature reigns supreme.

Every city has parks that you can go to and spend time in, and many have trees planted along streets. A back yard or a man-made lake may create a haven for you in which you can feel nature. Look for birds' nests or spider webs to show you where the nature hides. Find a place that connects you to nature that you can visit on your lunch break or before work each day.

My own favorite natural spot near my workplace is the top of a parking garage: this might sound strange, but I am able to watch the sunrise, unobstructed by buildings, each morning, and do devotionals there if sunrise comes around the time I'm due at work.

If you live in the country, you probably already know a place you can go to connect with the land. If you don't, look around. Hunt until you find a spot that speaks to you.

We do recommend that you think about your climate when you're looking for a nature spot. If it's getting to be winter at this point (and a large number of people start at Samhain, so it could be), remember that you'll want to think about that before picking a spot that is overly cold and wet, or hard (or dangerous!) to get to in the snow. If your climate is too cold, you might consider seeking out a greenhouse or conservatory for your nature meditation (though we recommend getting outside as much as the tips of your ears can stand).

Remember, too, that you can experience nature while doing all sorts of seasonal work, from cutting the grass to weeding the garden to raking leaves to shoveling snow. When you're doing one of these tasks that so many of us hate to do, stop and think about how it fits in with the cycles of nature. The simple act of working *in* nature can be remarkably fulfilling.

Also, consider your local parks, and schedule one weekend each month to spend some "outside time," either hiking, jogging, picnicking, or just doing activities in a natural space.

Once you have found this spot, go to it at least once per week for a full hour. Sit, stand, or lie in your place and simply feel the world around you. Isolate the call of a bird and concentrate on it. Listen for the sound of a lizard scurrying through the brush. Watch a colony of ants pick up food from an unsuspecting picnicker. Concentrate on these things, and ignore the machines and the other people around you: you'll have time for them later. Now, it's time for you to listen to Nature's Call.

Homework:

In your Dedicant Notebook, discuss what you felt when you were experiencing Nature. Did you have problems focusing? Did you have trouble finding your spot? Try drawing a map from your house or your office to this spot, but don't include street names or man-made objects; instead, use natural landmarks to remind yourself how to get there in the future (it doesn't have to be a very artistic map: I'll include a map of this sort from my house to my office to prove that sophistication is not a requirement at all). Were you able to hear things you've never heard before? Did you catch a glimpse of the Earth Mother playing with children in the park?

Example: Mapping with Natural Landmarks

My own process of creating a map from Point A to Point B shows just how non-artistic you can be and still manage to complete this project. Here, I've created a map from my home to my office, using nothing but the natural features available. Four key features factor into this map:

1. Directions (North, South, East, West)
2. The Olentangy River
3. An old sycamore tree that has a lot of memory tied up in it

4. A young oak tree that stands next to my office building

The map is really designed for me: it would be hard for another person to tell which sycamore, or which oak is referred to. But this isn't about helping others find the space: it's about how you, yourself, interact with nature in an attempt to connect with it.

So try the exercise. Be free with your mapping. Help yourself to orient your cosmos.

My Map:

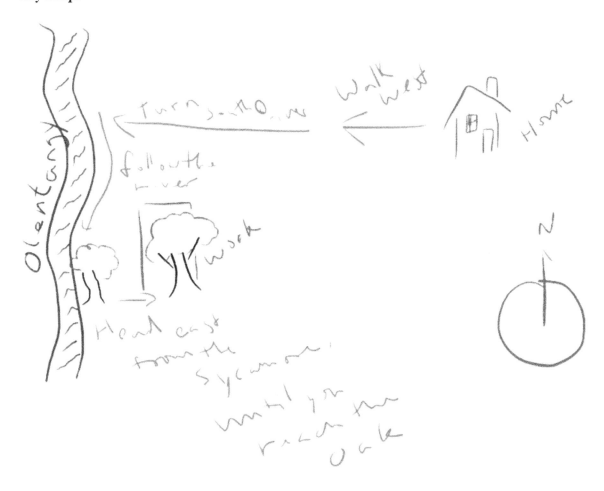

Week 6: First book started: I-E Studies

Related to Requirement: #3 – Book Reviews
Required Reading:

- *Our Own Druidry*, p. 17 - 18 (Concerning the Reading of Books)
- *Our Own Druidry*, Appendix B, p. xii - xiii (writing a book review)
- Start on one book from the list of IE titles at the ADF Website, A Recommended Reading List:
  <https://www.adf.org/training/resources/reading.html>

One of the reasons many people come to ADF is because they are looking for a religion or organization that is interested in both piety and study. Because this is a rare combination in the Neo-Pagan community, we are very proud to offer such things. We do expect our Dedicants to be well-versed in the basic scholarship behind ADF, the modern Neo-Pagan movement, and the historical roots of Neo-Paganism in general.

To this end, three book reviews are asked of all Dedicants: one Indo-European studies title (because ADF is an Indo-European based organization), one general Neo-Pagan movement book (because we are Neo-Pagan), and one book on one of the Indo-European hearth cultures (generally the hearth culture that the Dedicant will choose to work with).

We will work on the Indo-European title first in order to give you a broad exposure to all the potential hearth cultures ADF generally works in. The main idea is that if you are currently undecided about a hearth culture, this might help point you in the right direction. If you have decided on a hearth culture, then this will help you understand the similarities and differences between your hearth culture and others in the IE family.

As we do not expect you to finish the book you choose in one week, we will give you questions to think about now, and will remind you occasionally throughout the coming weeks to continue reading. **The book review for this title will be due on week 25.**

Remember to start all book reviews with the bibliographical information, such as an MLA citation[3]. What is the book about? Is there a main thesis? Can you summarize the main points? Why was this book on the reading list? Do you think it should be there? Does it inform your own personal practice in any way? Does it give you new ideas, crazy thoughts, or open your mind? Could you recommend this book to others? Do you have trouble understanding it, or is it a breeze? Are there things that would make it better?

Making an outline or notes as you read will be invaluable to writing your book review later.

Keep these questions in mind as you read through the book, and let your mentor know what you're reading so he or she can help answer any questions you might have!

Also, continue visiting the spot that helps keep you connected to Nature. You might make notes in your Dedicant Notebook about what you see, or if there are animals that appear often or plants that strike you as intriguing or odd.

---

[3] You can find a lot of help creating MLA citations at the Purdue OWL site:
https://owl.english.purdue.edu/owl/resource/747/01/

Week 7: Home Shrine

Related to Requirement: #4 – Home Shrine

Required Reading:

- *Our Own Druidry*: p. 87 - 92 (<u>Personal Work</u>)

Optional Reading:

- "<u>Placement of the Home Shrine</u>" by Rev. Michael J Dangler <<u>https://www.adf.org/members/training/dp/articles/placement-of-home-shrine.html</u>>;
- "<u>Creating the Desire for Worship</u>" by Rev. Michael J Dangler <<u>http://www.adf.org/articles/philosophy/creating-the-desire-for-worship.html</u>>;
- "<u>Takin' It All Home</u>" by Kami Landy <<u>http://www.adf.org/articles/identity/taking-it-all-home.html</u>>;
- *Sacred Fire, Holy Well* by Ian Corrigan, p. 77 – 79 ("Hallows of Worship," "Three Druidic Hallows"), & p. 86 – 88 ("The Shrine and the Nemeton");
- *The Solitary Druid* by Rev. Skip Ellison, p. 35 – 36 ("Walking the Talk")

One of the main components of the Path of an ADF Dedicant is to set up a home shrine. This shrine will become the center of your religious life, and is a visible reminder of the path you have chosen to take. It does not need to be elaborate, expensive, or set up in any specific way; rather, it should reflect you and your personal relationship with the deities and spirits. It can be cluttered with deity images, heaped with offerings, or a simple table with candles. The important thing is that it works for you.

You may wish to set up your shrine in such a way that it can double as a meditation seat (we will begin meditation next week), or you may wish to simply use the shrine as an altar upon which you will work daily devotionals or only use every six weeks for a High Day Rite. The usage and setup are entirely up to you.

Find a spot that is accessible to you for rites and/or meditation. You might set up a small table or hang shelves, or clear a bookshelf for the shrine. You might even set it up outside. Some people in very cramped houses with no available shelf space have painted their altars onto the wall. Place items that connect you to your deities, or that simply remind you of the spiritual connection you feel in ritual. You might represent the Fire, Well, and Tree from ADF liturgy, or perhaps the Gods, Ancestors, and Nature Spirits. Again, it's important to remember that this is your altar, and as such you should personalize it as much as you wish.

Something I found particularly helpful when doing my home shrine essays was to take a photograph of the shrine at each High Day. Doing this gives you the ability to revisit the process of building the shrine when you come back to write your final essay. If you can take pictures of the shrine more often, do that, too! You'd be surprised how much a shrine can change in just a couple of weeks if you're getting really active in your work.

Also, if you're looking for things to put on your shrine, check out both the ADF Store (http://store.adf.org/) and The Magical Druid (http://www.magicaldruid.com/, at a local festival, or in person in Columbus, OH). It's amazing what you can find out there.

Homework:

When you are satisfied (and remember that you can always work on it later!), grab a camera and snap a photo. Write down what is on the altar, how it looks, and why you chose the things you did. Think about how you would like to make it better, and brainstorm some suggestions. Keep these ideas in the back of your mind for later improvements to the shrine.

The author's first home shrine.
The title of the essay,
"Three Bowls and a Stick"
Makes more sense now, right?

Week 8: Meditation and Mental Training

Related to Requirement: #6 – Mental Training

Required Reading:

- *Our Own Druidry*, p. 37 – 38 ("Three Forms of Meditation")
- *Our Own Druidry,* p. 93 – 99 ("Druid Mental Training")

Optional Resources:

- Audio Meditations at the Three Cranes Grove, ADF, website: <http://threecranes.org/meditations/>
- Meditation for the Type A Personality by Jenni Hunt <http://www.adf.org/rituals/meditations/meditation-for-type-a.html>;
- Basic Meditation by Brenda Stumpp <http://www.adf.org/rituals/meditations/basic-meditation.html>;
- "Letting the World Slip Away" by Ladytoad <http://www.adf.org/rituals/meditations/letting-the-world-slip-away.html>;
- "Laughing Meditation" by Brandon Newberg, <http://www.adf.org/members/training/dp/articles/laughing-meditation.html>
- "An Anywhere Devotional" by Brandon Newberg <http://www.adf.org/rituals/general/anywhere-devotional.html>
- "Dual Trad Daily Devotionals" by Tanrinia, <http://www.adf.org/members/training/dp/articles/dual-trad-devotions.html>
- *Sacred Fire, Holy Well* by Ian Corrigan, p. 62 – 63 ("Meditation and Austerities"), & 89 – 97 ("The Power of Vision");
- *Training the Mind: Techniques of Trance and Meditation* CD/audio files by Ian Corrigan;
- *The Solitary Druid* by Rev. Skip Ellison, p. 36 – 40 ("Daily Devotionals" and "The Ritual Itself")

Suggested Audio

- Dedicant Meditation: "Seeking the Inner Grove" <http://threecranes.org/meditations/dpwoty/>

One of the keys to worship is the ability to directly enter a state in which you can correspond with the deities. Meditation is not simply a way of relaxing, but a way of connecting, and the end goal of whatever sort of mental training you do, from meditation to daily devotions, is that you become aware of the feeling of connection, and learn how to use it as a bridge in further ritual work.

There are several ways to fulfill this requirement in the DP, as there are several ways to build mental discipline. Listed here are just a few:

- *Passive Meditation:* Sitting, standing, or lying down, clearing the mind, and allowing thoughts to slide through.
- *Active Meditation:* Exercising, running, juggling, doing yoga, working a cash register, etc., in order to induce a meditative state.
- *Guided Meditation:* You can use a simple guided meditation script that you have prepared yourself, or that others have prepared for you. You can find many guided meditations that work in our cosmology, as well as meditaitons from many voices (both male and female) at the Three Cranes Grove, ADF, website: http://threecranes.org/meditations/
- *Daily Devotions:* Do a simple ritual each morning or night.
- *Daily Prayers:* Say a prayer on waking or on falling asleep, or over your lunch meal.
- *Trance Work:* Induce a trance, through any variety of methods.
- *Mantra Meditation:* In which you chant a simple mantra over and over until you manage to feel that connection.
- *Oracle meditation:* Pulling a rune, tarot card, or watching the flights of birds in order to gain some insight into your meditation. If you're interested in this particular kind of meditation, check out "Deepening Your Divination Practice," an hour-long workshop that will help you move deeper into the world of divination. On YouTube at: https://www.youtube.com/watch?v=OFNOH-UI3dI
- *Two Powers meditation:* Explained in week 11, it involves using the basic Two Powers meditation to connect with the currents of the world.

None of these are particularly right or wrong, but every person is different. It's important that you understand that you aren't stuck doing a single method of meditation that may or may not work for you.

If you already have a way that you meditate or induce trance, even if you've been doing it for ten years, it's a good idea to try something different, or to start over with basics. None of us is so good at being mentally disciplined that we would not benefit from starting over with the basics (even our past Archdruids, Rev. Kirk Thomas and Ian Corrigan, have said they "go back to basics" fairly often), and it's very important to remember that the wording of the requirement, "building mental discipline" implies that you will be advancing in your studies, and you are thus expected to show that you've learned something from this experience.

Many people have issues with finishing this requirement because it requires at least five months (23 weeks) of weekly practice (no, it does not require that you do this every day, but I assure you that more will be gained from doing your mental discipline every day). To that end, each week for the next 23 weeks, your homework will include a short description of what you've done over the past week. If you do this, by the end of this five-month period, you'll be completely done with your mental discipline requirement, as short summaries are all that's required.

At the end, we'll also ask you to write a short essay on this, which we encourage you to turn in. The essay will be mostly to help you see where you've been and where you're going, and we find that people who take the essay option are more likely to come to a solid understanding of their progress than those who do not.

Here are some pointers on completing the mental discipline requirement:

- You can do your mental discipline work once per day or once per week, or anything in between. I usually suggest that you start with a higher frequency than once a week, simply because you can then decide if it's too much, and you'll have a way to back off from meditation without accidentally falling off the horse. ***If you have a seven-day period during which you do no meditation between when you start and when you finish, you will need to re-start this requirement in order to pass.***

- Your frequency of doing this mental discipline building is also tied to your personal sense of piety: if you find it important to your definition of piety that a person do honor to the Kindred each day, then you will need to do that *for yourself*. If your definition of piety is more relaxed, and doing honor once a week is enough, then you might just do it every Thursday (or, if you prefer, "Thor's Day"). We *do* encourage you to push yourself, though, and go beyond what you might think is necessary.

- **Schedule a time to do this.** You'd be surprised how much easier it is to do your meditation or rites if they're set for specific times each day or each week. Try and make the time you do this about the same every day, and you'll start to notice that you begin to get into the "mood" for meditation around that time, too.

- Set a timer so you don't keep looking at your watch or the clock on the wall. Phase the timer out as you get a better feel for how long you've been doing it.

- **Start small.** Work with breathing first, and don't worry so much about getting connected. This is all about discipline, so learn to control your body first.

- Begin with a 10-minute meditation, or a very stripped-down version of the ritual you want to do. If you try too hard at first, you might accidentally turn yourself off to this completely. As with the above point, the trick is to "start small"

- If something doesn't work the first time, give it some time. People don't master meditation, ritual, or anything else their first time trying. Besides, if it doesn't work, you can only go up, and just putting forth the effort is important for showing improvement. A recommended minimum for this work might be 4 weeks: if it isn't working after 4 weeks of trying, feel free to move on to a different type of meditation.

- Popular breathing patterns include the 4-2-4-2 (breathe in for four, hold for two, out for four, hold for 2, repeat) and 4-4-4-4 (sometimes called a "square breathing pattern"). Once again, don't give up on the patterns after just one week: they take practice.

- Make sure you're comfortable, but not too comfortable! Sometimes, people spend the whole time thinking about how poorly the blood is circulating or about their keys sticking into their thigh; other times, people fall asleep!

- Get creative in your location: If meditating in front of a blank wall doesn't work, try meditating in front of your altar. If you're having trouble focusing, try staring at a candle flame. If you find yourself too tense, try meditating in the bathtub.
- **Make sure you're not disturbed.** Inform roommates and friends. Turn your phone off. Put a "Do Not Disturb" sign on your door. Meditate in the bathtub or shower if that's the only time you can get away from your family.
- Every time you do meditation or a devotional, write down your experiences in the meditation journal.

Hopefully, these tips will help get you started on basic meditation.

Homework:

Write about how your first week of meditation went. A couple of sentences will work. You might mention the breathing pattern you used, how long you did it, if anything happened, and any experiences you may have had. Don't get any more personal than you're comfortable being, and only let write down what you're comfortable with. See below for a real example of one of the author's meditation journal entries.

Also, continue visiting the spot that helps keep you connected to Nature. You might make notes in your Dedicant Notebook about what you see, or if there are animals that appear often or plants that strike you as intriguing or odd.

Suggested Exercise: "Seeking the Inner Grove"

One of the things each of us will learn to do is to create a centered experience in our minds, a place that is quiet and comfortable, where we can do the work of Our Druidry. Many of us have this "centered" place within us, and it's important to know how to find that Inner Grove when you do work as an ADF Dedicant. In addition, the process of building and maintaining an Inner Grove is required for ADF's Initiate Path, so this will give you a leg up on that, too!

There are many ways to an Inner Grove, but we've recorded a few options for people to work from. Over the course of this meditation requirement, we'll provide some guided meditations that you can use to help both locate and expand your own personal Inner Grove. You will find each of these meditations, organized by week, on the Three Cranes Grove, ADF, website, here: <http://threecranes.org/meditations/dpwoty/> The first meditation in this series is "Seeking the Inner Grove," under the "Week 8" heading.

Example: Meditation Journal Entry

Date: 02-17-2016, 7 AM

"Today, I spent 13 minutes listening to the Inner Grove guided meditation and doing work around that Grove. I began with some square breathing (4-4-4-4 counts), and moved on to the meditation once I felt centered. I could kind of see the Grove in the mist, but I was also a little bit distracted today, and had some trouble focusing on my place in the trees.

After I finally managed to get everything to come together, I spent a bit more time watching my breath. I started to feel centered here, and I had a good experience of that "silence" that the DP manual mentions. I felt good, calm, and in control. I came out of it feeling better than I did last week, so I feel like I'm improving."

Week 9: The second High Holy Day: an explanation.

Related to Requirement: #2 – Meaning and Discussion of High Days

Required Reading:
- *Our Own Druidry*, p. 60 – 72 (Hearth Cultures & High Days)
- *ADF Constitution*, Article 4
- *The ADF Core Order of Ritual for High Days*, <http://www.adf.org/rituals/explanations/core-order.html>

Optional Reading:
- *Our Own Druidry*, p. 49 – 73 (The Very Basics of Ritual);
- *Appendix 1: Resources and Rituals for the Wheel of the Year* in this book;
- Step by Step through a Druid Worship Ceremony, <http://www.adf.org/rituals/explanations/stepbystep.html>;
- The "Liturgy and Rituals" section of the ADF page, <http://www.adf.org/rituals/>
- The Three Cranes Grove, ADF, outline of ritual (with example prayers), <http://www.threecranes.org/liturgy/>
- *The Crane Breviary and Guide Book* from the Order of the Crane: <https://www.adf.org/system/files/members/orders/crane/print/cbgb-preview.pdf>
- Rev. Skip Ellison's *The Solitary Druid*, appropriate high day in Chapters 6 & 7
- Nicholas Egelhoff's *Sunna's Journey: Norse Liturgy Through the Wheel of the Year*, appropriate High Day description

Welcome to your second High Holy Day as an ADF Dedicant. Next week's lesson will be a recap of the rite you do for this holiday.

If your culture does not celebrate a specific feast, remember that most cultures had a festival or feast that would have been similar in intent and form, but it may have been celebrated at a different time of year. Unfortunately, much of the work of discovering which festival might match up to which High Day must be left to the individual Dedicant. Your mentor, of course is available for some help, but we urge you to seek out one of the culture-specific email lists to ask questions on. Quite often, they will be of more help than your mentor can be.

A lot of the High Holy Days are obviously agrarian-based. If the High Day feels "irrelevant," seek out relevance. Can you find the rhythms of nature in the city? Look hard for them, and I'll bet you can find something fresh and new in your climate that corresponds with this season.

Homework:

Now, in your Dedicant Notebook, reflect on this High Holy Day. Consider how it is celebrated in your hearth culture, or across hearth cultures. Are there any myths that are celebrated in connection with this feast? If so, what are they, and how do they fit in? What does this holiday or time of year mean to you? Do you look forward to it? Are there secular aspects of the holiday that mean a lot to you, or perhaps holdovers or memories of your childhood that you cherish? How do you know when this day arrives? Do you look at the calendar, or do you just *know* it has come? If you have children (or wish to have children), what key traditions do you wish to pass down to them? What, if anything, is spiritual or religious to you about this High Day or time of year, and how do you show that? Are there any traditions that your Grove has for this High Day? Finally, is there anything else about this holiday that you would like to add?

There, you've just written your second essay on a High Holy Day!

If you have a local Grove that you attend, then you should already have a rite you can attend. If you are solitary (and even if you do have a Grove, we still recommend), though, you will need to write and perform your own ritual for this rite. Because only four High Days are required to be done as ADF rituals, you don't need to be too concerned with exactly how to do an ADF rite, but you should certainly have something written up, or else go to the ADF website and find a ritual that will fit your hearth culture and use that. We do not expect you to be a skilled liturgist this early in the journey. Make sure that you have a rite ready before you intend to do the ritual, though, because last minute ritual writing is never fun for anyone.

See Appendix 1 for more information on what the High Day is about, where we have provided a number of links to help you think about the High Days themselves (and included places to find some example rituals for you to work from!)

Also, continue visiting the spot that helps keep you connected to Nature. You might make notes in your Dedicant Notebook about what you see, or if there are animals that appear often or plants that strike you as intriguing or odd.

Finally, write about your second week of meditation: experiences, breath pattern, difficulties. . . all these things are good to write down.

Week 10: Second High Day recap

Related to Requirement: #8 – High Days Attended
Required Reading: None.

You've made it through your second ritual, which means you're a quarter of the way through the wheel of the year with your Dedicant studies! Congratulations! It's now time to add to your essays for the Dedicant Path documentation by writing a recap of the rite!

Homework:

First, we've provided a sort of ritual write-up template that will help you get all the commonly needed details down in Appendix 2. You cannot just turn in a number of those sheets and expect to pass this requirement, though: you need to be much more in-depth. So grab some paper and start thinking about the rite by asking some good questions.

Let's start out with an easy one: how did the rite go in terms of structure? What things went wrong during the ritual? What things went right? Who were the patrons of the rite, and who was the gatekeeper? Did you have problems with saying the words without stumbling, or did everything come out smoothly? Did you forget to bring a sacrifice? Were you alone, or with a group? If you were with a group, did you say anything or do anything? Now, for the not so easy part: how did the rite go in terms of function and feeling? Did you feel anything during the ritual? Did you experience doubt or confidence? Can you describe what happened? If you were with a group, what did the other people say about what happened? What omens were drawn (if any), and what did they tell you? Could you feel the presence of any deities, spirits, or powers? What else about the rite struck you, or do you want to share?

If you answer those questions, you've just finished another essay for the Dedicant Path documentation!

Also, make sure you're still reading your Indo-European studies book, and taking notes as you go. The notes will help greatly when you go to write your review.

Finally, write about your third week of meditation: experiences, breath pattern, difficulties, successes. . . all these things are good to write down.

Week 11: The Two Powers

Related to Requirement: #5 – Two Powers; #6 – Mental Training
Required Reading:
- *Our Own Druidry*, p. 26 – 27 ("The Two Powers");
- *Our Own Druidry*, p. 36 – 37 ("The Two Powers")

Optional Reading and Resources:
- Two Powers Audio file:
  https://www.adf.org/system/files/members/training/dp/twopowers.mp3;
- "Two Powers Active Meditation" by Tommy Watson,
  <http://www.adf.org/rituals/meditations/2powers-active.html>
- *A Book of Pagan Prayer* by Ceisiwr Serith (ISBN: 1578632552) p. 34 – 39
  ("Creating a Sacred Space");
- *Sacred Fire, Holy Well* by Ian Corrigan, pgs. 11 ("Two Kinds of Magical
  Power"), 99 – 101 ("A Trance Attunement to the Underworld" & "A Trance
  Attunement to the Heavens");
- *The Solitary Druid* by Rev. Skip Ellison, p. 138 – 139 ("Two Power Meditation
  – Earth and Sky")

Suggested Audio
- Simple Two Powers Meditation: <http://threecranes.org/media/MJD-Two-
  Powers-Meditation.mp3>
- Shawneen's Two Powers Meditation:
  <http://threecranes.org/media/shawneen-two-powers.mp3>
- *Training the Mind: Techniques of Trance and Meditation* CD/audio by Ian Corrigan,
  "The Two Powers Exercise" and the introduction and discussion tracks

In every ADF group ritual, there is an attunement, designed to help put you in touch with the basic cosmology that ADF rituals work in. Many people use this particular attunement in their personal daily practice, as well. It is called the Two Powers meditation.

We mentioned the Two Powers a couple of weeks ago when we went over meditation, but said it would be explained this week. The reason we chose to present it this way is because for the beginner, it's important to understand how you breathe and how you can open up best in order to fully understand this meditation.

The Two Powers meditation is designed to put you in touch with the common (or "generic") Indo-European cosmic picture. This picture is composed of two axes: a horizontal axis and a vertical axis.

Along the vertical axis, you will find four things in this meditation:

- **The Underworld**: The deep earth, broad and cosmic, containing cooling underground streams, hot magma, and the world of our ancestors and the Chthonic deities.

- **The Midrealm**: The world as we know it, the domain of the Spirits and Deities of Nature and the world of the living.
- **The Upperworld**: Beyond the high reaches of the dome of the sky, a place of heroic Ancestors and Shining Ones.
- **The Center**: The point the self stands at the center of all the worlds.

Along the horizontal axis, there are four things you will find in this particular meditation:

- **The Land**: The land extends out around you while in ritual.
- **The Sea**: The sea supports and surrounds the land. The land actually floats on the sea, and by digging down into the earth you will eventually come into contact with those dark waters beneath it.
- **The Sky**: the sky reaches out above us, the shining dome of heaven. It encompasses everything.
- **The Center**: The tree, fire, door, pillar, or self stands at the center of all the worlds, the *axis mundi*.

This is summed up quite nicely in two prayers by Ceisiwr Serith:

> **The waters support and surround me.**
> **The land extends about me.**
> **The sky reaches out above me.**
> **At the center burns a living flame.**

And:

> **World below, watery world, with chaos and order overflowing.**
> **bring true creation into my life, with order and beauty,**
> **with power and grace.**
> **World above, far-flung heavens, ordering the world with might and law,**
> **bring true stability to my life, with law and structure,**
> **with clarity and reason.**
> **World about me, far-extending, with land well-set,**
> **bring true being into my life, with help and love,**
> **with health and prosperity.**

These prayers come from Ceisiwr's *A Book of Pagan Prayer* (p. 36-37), and they are very useful for working through the Two Powers when you don't want to do a whole long script like the one presented in *Our Own Druidry*.

The Two Powers meditation begins with simple relaxation. I always encourage people to try relaxing whenever they get the chance. You never know when the practice will be useful, right?

There are two currents (which is why this meditation is also often called the "Two Currents Meditation") at work here, which you will probably see immediately upon reading the meditation. The first is the Earth Power, described in our basic 2P meditation as cool, soothing, and nourishing. This is the fertile power of creativity, the chaos of potential from which ideas and thought-forms spring. It rises up through your body, pooling in the places where there are three cauldrons: one of fertility, one of healing and caring, and one of wisdom and vision. The earth power then rises up through your head and pours out your hands, returning to the Earth from whence it came, replenishing and recirculating this Earth Power through you over and over again.

The other current is the Sky Power. This comes from deep within the wheel of the sky, shining down onto you. It is described as warm, bright, and electric. It is ordered, as are the progressions of the stars in the night sky, or the sun through the day; this is where the thought-forms and the ideas become solid and ordered. The light meets the waters, mingling and reflecting on them. The waters shine as they flow through you, as the Sky Power mingles with the Earth Power, becoming part of the return flow to the earth as the waters flow from your hands and from the crown of your hands back to the earth. The Sky and the Earth meet in the three cauldrons, and the brightness of each is incredible.

This is the raw material of magic: the chaos of potential from the waters in the deep sea, and the order of the stars from the sky above. They meet in you, standing on the land. You are the crossroads, and you are the center. You might see yourself as the world tree, Yggdrasil; or perhaps as the cosmic pillar that holds the sky above the earth, or the fire whose smoke supports the heavens.

In Groves, the end of this attunement is often accompanied by a "mingling of waters," in which each person in a circle will reach out to the others, and the waters that well up from the earth and pour out the hands of the attendees will run together, and the shining light of each person's star will shine on all. It can be a truly powerful experience.

When you are finished with the Two Powers meditation, you may find yourself at the center of all things: the three realms of Land, Sea, and Sky; and the three worlds of Heavens, Midworld, and Underworld. These two axes meet within you, as a single point, with access to the entire cosmos.

We have provided the text of the Two Powers here, but there are also several audio Two Powers mediations on the ADF site (one is listed in the resources for this week's lesson). You may wish to record your own version, too.

Two Powers meditation text

(From p. 95 of the DP handbook; audio available on the ADF site, or the Three Cranes site)

Begin, O seeker of wisdom, with your breath... breathe deeply, from your belly... in... and out... make your body comfortable... stretch if you need to, settle in place... and focus on your breath... observe your breath as it flows in and out of your body... and with each breath, allow your body to relax... let your breath carry away tension from your flesh.. relaxing your feet and legs... letting your belly soften and relax... breathing away tension from your shoulders and arms... from your neck... relaxing your face and mouth, your eyes... with each breath your body becoming warmer, comfortable and relaxed... your mind alert and prepared for magic...

Now, with your body still and calm, imagine that from your feet, or the base of your spine, roots begin to grow downward... roots reaching and growing into the earth, down through soil and stone... deepening and spreading... reaching to touch the waters under the Earth... the Earth current... the dark, cool, magnetic power that nourishes and sustains life... as your roots touch this current it is drawn in and up toward your body... your breath draws the Earth power upward... into your body... the invisible, magnetic power fills your legs, energizing and strengthening... waters rise from the earth, into your legs... rising... into your loins... and pooling in your loins, a cauldron of Earth power... You breathe the power upward... rising from the earth, through your loins, rising up your spine... into your heart... pooling and filling a cauldron in your heart with healing, restoring energy... power rising from the deep, through your loins, through your heart... rising up your spine and into your head... filling a cauldron of wisdom and vision behind your eyes... and rising still, filling all your body and flowing out again through the crown of your head... through your hands... flowing out around your body and back into the earth... the power under the Earth flows in you... grounding you in the source of life...

Now imagine the sky overhead... The sun and moon and, far beyond them, the stars... imagine a single star at the center of the sky, shining directly over your head... the center of your inner sky, your own pole-star...see a flash of light shining down from that star... streaming down between moon and sun... gold, silver and blue-white light... the bright, warm, electric power of the sky... the light touches your head, filling and illuminating the cauldron like sun on still water... shining from above... filling your head with warm, awakening power... flowing down into your heart... warming the cauldron... shining down through head and heart, illumining the waters... downward to reach your loins... The cauldron shines with sky power in your loins... Tingling, electrical light in head, heart and loins... the light flows downward into Earth, and you are shining and flowing with the mingled powers of Earth and sky... the raw material of magic... the chaos of potential and the world order...

These powers are balanced in you... yours to shape and use... always with you in some degree... But for now, allow the powers to recede... waters to the Earth, light to the sky... knowing that each time you attune to them you become more attuned, more at one with the powers... breath deep... and allow your awareness to return to your common senses... as you open your eyes...

Homework:

Work through the Two Powers meditation. Work on getting the visualization down well, but don't be discouraged if you have a hard time with the visuals. Being able to see things sometimes takes time. If you cannot see everything, you might start with one current and then the other, and then try to mingle everything. You don't have to get it right the first time, nor do you have to see it all every time. This meditation takes practice, especially if you don't have someone to guide you through it the first couple of times. Keep in mind that there is a recording on the ADF webpage, and you can always record yourself reading it.

You should still be doing regular meditation practice: if you feel ready, you can do a Two Powers meditation in place of (or in addition to!) your current meditations. Either way, make sure you write a separate entry for meditation that you can send to your reviewer.

You might make entries in your meditation journal or small, short notes in your Dedicant Notebook, but don't write the essay on the Two Powers yet! We'll do that later (Week 30). The exit standard calls for an essay about your "understanding" of the Two Powers, and you'll understand it best if you have done some practice with it first.

Week 12: Ancestors, the Mighty Dead

Related to Requirement: #9 – Relationships to Kindred

Required Reading:

- *Our Own Druidry*, p. 120 – 121 ("Kindred Attunement Work")
- *Our Own Druidry*, p. 26 ("The Ancestors")

Optional Reading:

- "Ancestors Invocation" by Jennifer Ellison
  <http://www.adf.org/articles/gods-and-spirits/ancestors/invocation.html>
- "A Beginner's Guide to Genealogical Research: or How I Connected to My Ancestors" by Meghan E. M. <http://www.adf.org/articles/gods-and-spirits/ancestors/beginners-genealogical-research.html>
- "Ancestors For Those Without Ancestors" by Renee Rhodes
  <http://www.adf.org/members/training/dp/articles/without-ancestors.html>
- *The Solitary Druid* by Rev. Skip Ellison, p. 72 ("Ancestors")
- *Sacred Fire, Holy Well* by Ian Corrigan, p. 16 ("Ancestors"), p. 49 – 53 ("The Afterlife, the Heroes, and the Dead")

Optional Video

- *An Awfully Big Adventure: Signposts on the Soul's Journey Through the Indo-European Afterlife* by Rev. Michael J Dangler
  <https://www.youtube.com/watch?v=Szqz9Clyfa0>

"Humans are not proud of their ancestors, and rarely invite them round to dinner."

-Douglas Adams

The Ancestors begin our work with the Three Kindred: the Shining Ones (Deities), the Noble Ones (Nature Spirits), and the Mighty Ones (Ancestors). We honor the dead for a number of reasons, not the least of which is that we only exist because they did. When we think of ancestors, though, we might only think of our parents, or Great-Great-Grandpa Winston who told the greatest stories, or Grandma Olga who introduced us to folk magic.

Of course these would be the first people you would think of: they're blood-kin. But there are many types of Ancestors:

- **Blood-Kin**: These are ancestors of your blood, such as Grandpa Winston above, or your mother, or you sister, or your child. All of these are Ancestors, or would have been considered so by the Indo-European peoples.
- **Heart-Kin**: These are the close friends with whom there are ties of love, respect, and strong friendship. They are family, even if there is no blood tie.

- **Hearth-Kin**: These are people who have shared your hearth religion, though they may not be close friends or blood-relatives. (Also called "Spirit-Kin.")
- **Mentor-Kin**: These are teachers, guides, and friends with whom you share an intellectual lineage: perhaps you learned something from them that profoundly affected your life, or you are following in their footsteps in learning.

In any case, it is you who puts a person into each category, and it is you who chooses how to honor each of them.

What's that? You're not sure how to honor them? There are many ways to honor the dead.

- **Don't forget them.** Learn stories about their lives, either by asking them to tell the story, or by piecing it together through newspaper articles or second-hand accounts.
- Make an effort to put together a family tree of sorts. Organize it however you wish. Add in your friends and mentors, ancient Pagans you may idolize.
- Visit grave-sites and leave flowers or place flags on their graves if they were veterans.
- Remember them on secular holidays, such as Memorial Day.
- Set a place for them at your table each Samhain.
- Place a box on your altar, and fill it with things that remind you of your ancestors.
- Finally, tell the stories you know. The Norse often said that you didn't die until you were forgotten, so keep them alive through your words. A good story will travel forever.

People used to spend a lot of time in cemeteries. In the Victorian age, they would have picnic lunches near the graves of deceased relatives and would talk about them and tell stories. There is an innate human need to remember our dead, because we know that we will be one of them eventually.

Homework:

Think the Mighty Dead in your life. Do you remember stories that you like to tell? Does your family do anything special to commemorate those who have passed on? Do you think that your ancestors watch you? Consider how you think they would like to be honored. Write these things down in your Dedicant Notebook for future reference. Include some stories about your ancestors, maybe a photo or two.

Remember to keep visiting your site for observing nature. Have you noticed any changes as the seasons go by yet? Are there landscape changes? Do you feel a connection to the land? Write these in your Dedicant Notebook for reference, also.

Finally, write about your fifth week of meditation: experiences, breath pattern, difficulties. . . all these things are good to write down.

Week 13: The Nine Virtues: Wisdom

Related to Requirement: #1 – Nine Virtues
Required Reading:
- *Our Own Druidry*, p. 13 ("Virtue, Piety and Study" & "Nine Pagan Virtues");
- *Our Own Druidry*, p. 81-86 ("Lore and Essays")

Suggested Reading:
- A Virtuous Life Nine Virtues study guide by Rev. Michael J Dangler: <https://www.adf.org/system/files/members/training/dp/publications/dp-req-1-nine-virtues.pdf>

This is the first lesson on the Nine Pagan Virtues that ADF asks its Dedicants to understand (and thus also the longest lesson of the nine). Note the language here: we do not require you to follow a certain set of ethics or morals; rather, we request that you seriously examine and show an understanding of the Virtues that the Clergy Council of ADF has recommended for persons dedicated to Our Druidry. If there are Virtues that you do not agree with, then we encourage you to give reasons for that disagreement and to ask questions. We most emphatically do ***not*** want you to accept these Virtues (or any other teachings of ADF) without question. ADF is not a church that follows others without question, but a religion in which people ideally share civilized discourse and ask questions of each other.

The Nine Virtues are **wisdom, piety, vision, courage, integrity, perseverance, hospitality, moderation, and fertility**. Each of these will be examined in turn (beginning with wisdom this week), but first let us consider how we might use them in daily life.

The Virtues can be viewed in several ways. The first is that you can examine every decision in the light of these Virtues. Over time and with practice, this will become like second nature if you work at it, and you will start to ask yourself all the time if this or that action is "virtuous". Another option is to look at the Virtues as a tool for examining situations. In this method, rather than making every small decision be about piety or moderation, you can focus on a larger perspective and work through a group of decisions with a general idea of being "right" in your action. Finally, you can look at your whole life (or large chapters of it) and apply the Virtues to decisions that affect your whole life. Of course, you can also apply it to all these things at once. There is no real "correct" way to use the Virtues; they are simply signposts that can help guide you on your path through life.

You might notice that the Nine Virtues as a whole seem to group together into threes. The Nine Virtues themselves are actually a triad of three triads.

- **The first triad (wisdom, piety and vision)** relates to the first function of Indo-European societies, the priestly class, as postulated by Dumezil. These Virtues emphasize things that are acquired through spiritual endeavors, thoughtfulness, and openness. These three Virtues are the same as those we would expect of our spiritual leaders.

- **The second triad (courage, integrity and perseverance)** corresponds to the second function of IE societies, the warrior class. These virtues appear at first to emphasize the physical, but a warrior in the legends and cycles is never purely devoted to the strength of his or her arm. Often, they have the innate qualities of courage, integrity and perseverance that see them through the toughest times. These skills are learned on the battlefield and in the play-training that heroes receive in their youth, but it is off the battlefield that these skills are often honed. These particular Virtues require hard work to build into your life and work, but they are well worth it.

- **The third triad (hospitality, moderation and fertility)** relates to the third function of IE societies, the producing class. These are the farmers, artisans and healers of the ancient world, and it is with them that we find certain social contracts as virtues. Hospitality, for instance, is a contract between human and deity, and that contract must be respected for society to continue through its cycles. This set of Virtues is important to making and remaking the world throughout its cycles.

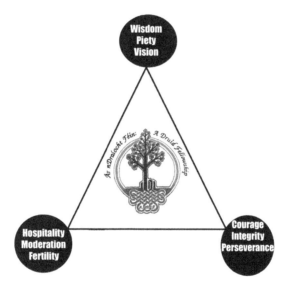

It must be stressed, the categorization of these Virtues into Triads is not the begin-all and end-all of the ways they can be applied, nor should it suggest that a priest has a set of virtues different from a warrior and different from a farmer: instead, all people in all classes of society should have virtues from each of these triads. What can piety be without hospitality, or integrity without wisdom?

Consider different ways to think on and divide up the Virtues listed here. In Three Cranes Grove, ADF, we sometimes divide them up mythically, along the lines of the myths that represent our name. Consider a grouping like this:

Esus (the god)	Trigaranus (the three cranes)	Tarvos (the bull)
Wisdom	Vision	Piety
Perseverance	Integrity	Courage
Moderation	Hospitality	Fertility

- *Esus* represents wisdom, perseverance, and moderation because he is the one who prunes the tree, who ensures that it grows straight and true.
- *Trigaranus* (the three cranes) are vision, integrity, and hospitality because they have a unique perspective, offer guidance and harbor lost souls, and are not afraid to speak the truth.
- *Tarvos* (the bull) is piety, courage, and fertility because the bull sacrifice is a pious act, the bull is a direct aspect of the fertility of the land and the folk, and Tarvos embodies courage.

How you see the virtues is important, but more important is your critical thought about how they interact within you and with the people around you. Think hard on them, and question them well.

Now that you have a basic overview of the Nine Virtues, we should move on to our first one, Wisdom.

Homework:

Our Own Druidry defines wisdom as follows: "Good judgment, the ability to perceive people and situations correctly, deliberate about and decide on the correct response."

Read through that statement until you think you understand it. In your Dedicant Notebook, answer the following questions: Does that definition cover wisdom in your eyes? Is it simply good judgment, or is there more to it?

If that definition doesn't quite sit right with you, head to your nearest dictionary and read the definitions in that it provides. Write it down (you will need to include a dictionary definition in your final write-up). Do any of those definitions make sense? Can they encompass all that wisdom is?

Now think of your own personal view of wisdom. Try to write it down in words. Feel free to steal phrases from the dictionary or the handbook if you need to. Can you come up with a definition of wisdom that makes good sense to you?

Now, think about people you know whom you would call "wise". Examine why you think of them that way: is it something they know, something they do, or something they have said? Is it something beyond this? Can you find words to describe it?

Think about myths and legends from different cultures. Did they have a deity for wisdom? What else was that deity a patron of? Was the deity male or female, do you place a gender value on wisdom, and does it surprise you to think of it in terms of a gender? Was there a character in a myth that showed real wisdom? How was that wisdom attained (in Irish lore for instance, the Salmon of Wisdom was the source for Fionn MacCumhail)?

Do you see yourself as wise? Wise in some ways but not others, perhaps? Not wise at all? Does one need to be wise to understand the concept of wisdom, or to wonder if something is wise? Can a wise choice be made by anyone? Can someone make a wise choice consciously?

Think of a time when you have exemplified this virtue. How did you feel? Did you know that this was a virtue at the time? Now think about a time when you failed to show this virtue. How did that make you feel? Did you feel as if you'd done something wrong or inadequate?

Finally, is wisdom a Virtue? Is it one that you agree should be on ADF's list? Why was it chosen? What is it about wisdom that either makes it a Virtue or keeps it from being one? If you have decided that it is not a Virtue, would you suggest another term, removing it altogether, or replacing it with something else entirely?

Now, go back through your answers to these questions and form a response of at least 125 words to "describe your understanding of the Virtue of wisdom."

And you have your first virtues essay out of the way!

Example: A Writing Process for a Virtue Essay

You might want to format your essay kind of like this:

1. Put the definition from the DP handbook and your dictionary definition at the top of the page.
2. Sum up your definition of the Virtue in a sentence or two. No more than that.
3. Respond to the definition in the DP handbook and the dictionary. Compare it to your own definition. What are one or two key differences or similarities? State them. Explain why you differ, or why you think you believe similarly.
4. Provide a short one- to two-sentence description of an experience you have had with this Virtue that illustrates your definition.
5. Are there important links to other Virtues, or links to our ritual structure? Mention those links here, and tell why they are important.

Week 14: The Home Shrine (revisited)

Related to Requirement: #4 – Home Shrine

Rather than assign reading, this week we're going to simply look at your Home Shrine to help you track the changes and maybe help give you some ideas.

First, take a picture. You'd be surprised how much your Home Shrine changes over time. If you still have the picture from week 7, compare it with the way your Shrine looks now. Has it changed at all? Are there things you have added or taken away or replaced?

Consider those things carefully. Why did you add this item? Why did you remove that one? What made this object more special to you than the last object that was on the altar?

Does it feel like there is something missing? Does something seem out of place? Is it just right?

How have you worked with it over the past seven weeks? Has the method of your working shaped the way the altar looks now, or does the way the altar looks affect the way you work? Are you happy with the location of the altar? Have you moved it in the past seven weeks? Do you plan on moving it in the future?

Now, what would you like to do to improve it? Write down your dreams, or sketch out your dream altar. Can you make it look like that? What do you need to do in order to make your altar look the way you want it?

Finally, consider how this shrine compares with the spot where you visit with nature. Do you feel that nature is accessible from this shrine? Or do you prefer to be outside in order to deal directly with nature? Are there ways to bring nature into your Home Shrine?

Homework:

Answer the above questions in your Dedicant Notebook. Continue work with the Two Powers attunement and your meditation. Visit the space where you connect to nature, and continue your nature meditations, too.

Suggested Exercise: "The Inner Grove: Seeking a Symbol"

Back in Week 8, we did an exercise to locate and experience your Inner Grove. This week, we're going to travel out from that Grove to seek something: a symbol for use on the journey we're taking.

Many paths lead outward from the center of our sacred Groves. This meditation will show you just one of them. This meditation is available on the Three Cranes Grove, ADF, website, here: <http://threecranes.org/meditations/dpwoty/> This is the second meditation in this series, "The Inner Grove: Seeking a Symbol," under the "Week 14" heading.

Week 15: The Nine Virtues: Piety

Related to Requirement: #1 – Nine Virtues

Required Reading:

- *Our Own Druidry*, p. 13 ("Virtue, Piety and Study" & "Nine Pagan Virtues");
- *Our Own Druidry*, p. 81-86 ("Lore and Essays")

Optional Reading:

- "Reintroducing Solitary Work into Your Life" by Rev. Michael J Dangler <http://www.adf.org/articles/solitary/reintroducing-solitary-work.html>
- A Virtuous Life Nine Virtues study guide by Rev. Michael J Dangler: <https://www.adf.org/system/files/members/training/dp/publications/dp-req-1-nine-virtues.pdf>
- "Where's the Belief? Piety in the DP" by Rev. Michael J Dangler <http://www.adf.org/members/training/dp/articles/wheres-the-belief.html>

Welcome to the second of the Nine Virtues, Piety! Piety is, of course, the second in the first triad I explained in week 13, the triad that corresponds to the priestly class. You might consider going back to read through Week 13's lesson to get a background if you have forgotten some of it.

Homework:

Our Own Druidry defines Piety as follows: "Correct observance of ritual and social traditions, the maintenance of the agreements (both personal and societal) we humans have with the Gods and Spirits. Keeping the Old Ways, through ceremony and duty."

Read through that statement until you think you understand it. In your Dedicant Notebook, answer the following questions: Does that definition cover piety in your eyes? Is it simply attending rites from a position of duty, or is there more to it?

What does the definition mean by "maintenance of agreements" and "duty"? Do these terms sit well with you?

If that definition doesn't quite sit right with you, head to your nearest dictionary and read the definitions in that it provides. Write it down (it is strongly recommended that you include a dictionary definition in your final write-up). Do any of those definitions make sense? Can they encompass all that piety is?

Now think of your own personal view of piety. Try to write it down in words. Feel free to steal phrases from the dictionary or the Handbook if you need to. Can you come up with a definition of piety that makes good sense to you?

Now, think about people you know whom you would call "pious". Examine why you think of them that way: is it something they know, something they do, or something they have said? Is it something beyond this? Can you find words to describe it?

Think about myths and legends from different cultures. How was piety shown in the myths and legends? Was there a character in a myth that showed real piety? How was that piety displayed (in Roman lore for instance, Aneas was often referred to as "pious Aneas")?

Do you see yourself as pious? Pious in some ways but not others, perhaps? Not pious at all? Does one need to be pious to understand the concept of piety, or to wonder if something is pious? Can a pious choice or action be made by anyone?

Think of a time when you have exemplified this virtue. How did you feel? Did you know that this was a virtue at the time? Now think about a time when you failed to show this virtue. How did that make you feel? Did you feel as if you'd done something wrong or inadequate?

Is piety something that is defined purely by actions (i.e. going through the motions), purely by intent (i.e. putting your heart into it), or both? Is one of these things more important than the other?

Finally, is piety a Virtue? Is it one that you agree should be on ADF's list? Why was it chosen? What is it about piety that either makes it a Virtue or keeps it from being one? If you have decided that it is not a Virtue, would you suggest another term, removing it altogether, or replacing it with something else entirely?

Now, go back through your answers to these questions and form a response of at least 125 words to "describe your understanding of the Virtue of piety."

And you have your second virtues essay out of the way!

Week 16: The third High Holy Day: an explanation

Related to Requirement: #2 – Meaning and Discussion of High Days
Required Reading:
- *Our Own Druidry*, p. 60 – 72 (Hearth Cultures & High Days)
- *ADF Constitution*, Article 4
- *The ADF Core Order of Ritual for High Days*,
  <http://www.adf.org/rituals/explanations/core-order.html>

Optional Reading:
- *Our Own Druidry*, p. 49 – 73 (The Very Basics of Ritual);
- *Appendix 1: Resources and Rituals for the Wheel of the Year* in this book;
- Step by Step through a Druid Worship Ceremony,
  <http://www.adf.org/rituals/explanations/stepbystep.html>;
- The "Liturgy and Rituals" section of the ADF page,
  <http://www.adf.org/rituals/>
- The Three Cranes Grove, ADF, outline of ritual (with example prayers),
  <http://www.threecranes.org/liturgy/>
- *The Crane Breviary and Guide Book* from the Order of the Crane:
  <https://www.adf.org/system/files/members/orders/crane/print/cbgb-preview.pdf>
- Rev. Skip Ellison's *The Solitary Druid*, appropriate high day in Chapters 6 & 7
- Nicholas Egelhoff's *Sunna's Journey: Norse Liturgy Through the Wheel of the Year*, appropriate High Day description

Welcome to your third High Holy Day as an ADF Dedicant. Next week's lesson will be a recap of the rite you do for this holiday.

If your culture does not celebrate a specific feast, remember that most cultures had a festival or feast that would have been similar in intent and form, but it may have been celebrated at a different time of year. Unfortunately, much of the work of discovering which festival might match up to which High Day must be left to the individual Dedicant. Your mentor, of course is available for some help, but we urge you to seek out one of the culture-specific email lists to ask questions on. Quite often, they will be of more help than your mentor can be.

The eight High Days are outlined on pages 60 – 72 of *Our Own Druidry*. If you are not of a Celtic hearth culture or you simply wish to expand your horizons and try a different culture because you are unsure what to do, locate a ritual that seems appropriate, where it gives a short description of the feast. Take that description and work to find a compatible feast in your hearth culture for that particular High Day.

A lot of the High Holy Days are obviously agrarian-based. If the High Day feels "irrelevant," seek our relevance. Can you find the rhythms of nature in the city? Look hard for them, and I'll bet you can find something fresh and new in your climate that corresponds with this season.

Homework:

Now, in your Dedicant Notebook, reflect on this High Holy Day. Consider how it is celebrated in your hearth culture, or across hearth cultures. Are there any myths that are celebrated in connection with this feast? If so, what are they, and how do they fit in? What does this holiday or time of year mean to you? Do you look forward to it? Are there secular aspects of the holiday that mean a lot to you, or perhaps holdovers or memories of your childhood that you cherish? How do you know when this day arrives? Do you look at the calendar, or do you just *know* it has come? If you have children (or wish to have children), what key traditions do you wish to pass down to them? What, if anything, is spiritual or religious to you about this High Day or time of year, and how do you show that? Are there any traditions that your Grove has for this High Day? Finally, is there anything else about this holiday that you would like to add?

There, you've just written another essay on a High Holy Day, and you're still in the first half of your training!

If you have a local Grove that you attend, then you should already have a rite you can attend. If you are solitary (and even if you do have a Grove, I still recommend), though, you will need to write and perform your own ritual for this rite. Because only four High Days are required to be done as ADF rituals, you don't need to be too concerned with exactly how to do an ADF rite, but you should certainly have something written up, or else go to the ADF website and find a ritual that will fit your hearth culture and use that. We do not expect you to be a skilled liturgist this early in the journey. Make sure that you have a rite ready before you intend to do the ritual, though, because last minute ritual writing is never fun for anyone.

See Appendix 1 for more information on what the High Day is about, where we have provided a number of links to help you think about the High Days themselves (and included places to find some example rituals for you to work from!)

Also, continue visiting the spot that helps keep you connected to Nature. You might make notes in your Dedicant Notebook about what you see, or if there are animals that appear often or plants that strike you as intriguing or odd.

Finally, write about your eighth week of meditation: experiences, breath pattern, and difficulties . . . all these things are good to write down.

Week 17: Third High Day recap

Related to Requirement: #8 – High Days Attended
Required Reading: None.

You've made it through your third ritual, which means you're well on your way through the wheel of the year with your Dedicant studies! Congratulations! It's now time to add to your essays for the Dedicant Path documentation by writing a recap of the rite!

Homework:

First, we've provided a sort of ritual write-up template that will help you get all the commonly needed details down in Appendix 2. You cannot just turn in a number of those sheets and expect to pass this requirement, though: you need to be much more in-depth. So grab some paper and start thinking about the rite by asking some good questions.

Let's start out with an easy one: how did the rite go in terms of structure? What things went wrong during the ritual? What things went right? Who were the patrons of the rite, and who was the gatekeeper? Did you have problems with saying the words without stumbling, or did everything come out smoothly? Did you forget to bring a sacrifice? Were you alone, or with a group? If you were with a group, did you say anything or do anything? Now, for the not so easy part: how did the rite go in terms of function and feeling? Did you feel anything during the ritual? Did you experience doubt or confidence? Can you describe what happened? If you were with a group, what did the other people say about what happened? What omens were drawn (if any), and what did they tell you? Could you feel the presence of any deities, spirits, or powers? What else about the rite struck you, or do you want to share?

If you answer those questions, you've just finished another essay for the Dedicant Path documentation!

Also, make sure you're still reading your Indo-European studies book, and taking notes as you go. The notes will help greatly when you go to write your review.

Week 18: Personal Religion

Related to Requirement: #10 – Personal Religion; #9 – Relationships to Kindred

Required Reading:

- *Our Own Druidry*, p. 17 ("The Hearth Oath")
- *Our Own Druidry*, p. 117 – 122 ("Personalizing Your Paganism")
- *Our Own Druidry*, p. xv – xvi ("Appendix 1: Adapting the DP to Specific Ethnic Paths")

Optional reading:

- *Our Own Druidry*, p. 60 – 72 ("Hearth Cultures and High Days")
- *Our Own Druidry*, p. xvii – xxvii ("Using the DP for Grove Building");
- Reintroducing Solitary Work into Your Life by Rev. Michael J Dangler <http://www.adf.org/articles/solitary/reintroducing-solitary-work.html>
- "Ratri" by Adhitin Ratrija <http://www.adf.org/articles/gods-and-spirits/vedic/ratri.html>
- "The Case for Choosing a Pantheon" by Ian Corrigan <http://www.adf.org/articles/gods-and-spirits/general/case-for-choosing-a-pantheon.html>
- "Dual Trad Daily Devotionals" by Tanrinia, <http://www.adf.org/members/training/dp/articles/dual-trad-devotions.html>

Perhaps the least defined (and yet most intriguing) requirement in the documentation is number 10: "A brief account of the efforts of the Dedicant to develop and explore a personal (or Grove-centered) spiritual practice, drawn from a specific culture or combination of cultures."

This particular requirement looks easy at first blush, yet there is an air of difficulty about it. For some Dedicants who already know where they're going, this might be simple to explain. For others who have started out on this Path with no clear focus to their worship, it might prove extremely difficult.

We've already started down this path in our first week, when we talked some about why you were doing this. The second week, we talked a bit about your first oath.

First, let's return to those questions we asked in Week One. Get out your Dedicant Notebook and find the page that had those questions:

- Why have you chosen to undertake the Dedicant Path?
- Is this a step on your path, or will this become the path itself?
- What do you expect to learn?
- What would you like to get out of this journey?
- Do you know where this path will take you?
- If you have just joined ADF, why have you chosen to work on this immediately?

- If you have been in ADF for a long time, why are you starting only now?
- Does it look hard or easy?
- Which requirements appear to be difficult to you now, and which appear to be easy?
- Do you have doubts, questions, or concerns that I can help you with?

Are the answers to these questions still the same? Are you finding this course of study harder, or easier than it was at first? Are you starting to get what you wanted out of this path? Are there nagging questions that you need answered?

Now, go take a look at your First Oath. Do you feel that you are upholding that Oath? Are there ways to better observe it? Did you make any mistakes in the way you wrote it? Are you still comfortable with it?

It is good to reflect on the First Oath from time to time. It is an excellent gauge of your progress and your drive to finish this.

If you didn't already come into ADF with a strong leaning toward a culture or many cultures, now is the time to seriously begin examining them. The reason that we've started you out with the Indo-European studies title is that we wanted you to get a feel for the various cultures out there that ADF is able to help you represent. Hopefully, by now you've gotten at least a short overview of the main cultures within the I-E spectrum, and have started looking closely at one or two of them. (If you haven't, that's okay, too. There are several ADF members and Groves that focus on "eclectic" worship as their "hearth culture".)

Even if you did have a strong leaning toward one culture when you started with ADF, I hope that the I-E studies title you have been reading has opened your eyes to new ways of looking at these cultures.

What is important now, though, is to start thinking (if you have not already) about what culture (or cultures) are resonating with you. Is there a specific culture that is calling out to you? Or perhaps you've stumbled across a deity that seems to have made you his or her own? Are you having trouble deciding between two, or perhaps three?

What ADF's hearth cultures allow you to do is "personalize" your Paganism. It gives you the opportunity to look at the sea of religions out there, choose one particular culture, pantheon, or deity, and devote yourself to that totally, or to turn in completely the opposite direction and shout out, "I'm not going to be placed inside a single box! I'm going to choose my deities as one would choose colours for a painting, mixing and matching as I see fit to form a beautiful picture of my world!" Both directions are valid, and both can be very powerful experiences.

If you are totally unsure where to begin, this week's required reading in *Our Own Druidry* gives a lot of useful information. Suggestions include study and meditation, divination, visionary experiences, and conscious choice. There is nothing that says you need to find a pantheon or Patron deity now; indeed, sometimes waiting for the right patron or pantheon to show up can take years. Likewise, there is nothing to say that it hasn't already happened to you, and you just need to look for the signs if you don't already know it.

[*A note on the word "Patron"*: Some members of ADF use the word "Matron" to describe a female deity that acts as Patron. If you are more comfortable with this, then please feel free to use it. The word "Patron", though, was chosen because of its dictionary definition. This definition has nothing to do with gender, but with the type of relationship that a "Patron" provides: it is one in which someone with more grants blessings or boons to another who does not have the means to provide them to him/herself. The root may come from a masculine word in Latin, but that does not mean that all Patrons are male. But again, it is personal choice, and we encourage you to consider yourself free to refer to your deities as you or they prefer.]

In the original revision of the Dedicant Path, we expected our Dedicants to begin seeking a Patron deity before they finished the DP. This turned out to be a mistake in general, because many people were so new that they didn't even have a hearth culture, or else they had been working so long with a Patron that they couldn't remember the process of finding him or her. Now, Patronage is summed up under this requirement, "seeking personal religion." If you have a Patron, or think you do, now may be a good time to begin to build that relationship. If you are unsure or don't think you have one yet, give it time. It may take years before one comes out to meet you at the boundaries and be named, but if there is a Patron, he, she, or they will find you.

Homework:

Write about your feelings regarding your First Oath in your Dedicant Notebook. Answer the questions about it above. Also, compare where you are now with your answers from the first week. Write about any feelings you have or changes you would make to the answers you gave.

Write down your feelings on Hearth Culture. Do you think you have one? Do you know you have one? What makes you so certain, and what makes you still feel a bit insecure? What do you like about the culture(s), if you have chosen one or two? What do you dislike about them? If you are unsure about your cultures, would it help to do a compare/contrast chart to weigh several cultures against one another? Try it and see.

Finally, is there a pantheon that you have heard calling you? Is there a specific Patron? How do you feel about the word "Patron" itself? Does it fit the way you think about deity? Is there a single Patron, or are there many? Do you know anything about this particular deity (or group of deities)?

Remember to continue your meditation, and go to your special spot in nature. And of course, keep reading your I-E studies book!

Week 19: The Dedicant Oath: First Thoughts

Related to Requirement: #11 – Dedicant Oath and Rite

Required Reading:

- *Our Own Druidry*, p. 123 – 128 ("The Dedicant's Oath")

Optional Reading:

- Rev. Michael J Dangler's Dedicant Oath, <http://www.chronarchy.com/mjournal/oath/>;
- Raven Mann's Dedicant Oath, <http://www.adf.org/members/training/dp/examples/raven-mann/oath-rite.html>
- Monika's Dedicant Oath, <https://www.adf.org/members/training/dp/articles/dedicant-oath-monika.html>
- Narabali's Dedicant Oath, <https://www.adf.org/members/kins/eastern-gate/vedic-oath.html>

What is the Dedicant Oath? How does it work? What does it mean? Why do we require one for our Dedicants?

The Dedicant Oath is really the crowning achievement in the Dedicant Path. We're discussing it now so that you have ample time to occasionally re-visit the idea before the time to take it arrives. The Dedicant Oath will be done at the end of our journey toward ADF Dedicant status, but it will be up to you to decide whether this Oath is the end of your journey, or the beginning of a new one.

Oaths are often tricky things to write. Oaths are binding, creating a bargain between you and the Kindred. Because of this, you need to be very precise in your wording. That's why we're looking at what you might want to say now, hardly halfway through the year, and we'll look again later.

The Dedicant Oath is not meant to be a "pledge of allegiance" to ADF, the Archdruid, or your Grove. Also, this Oath is not meant to be a patronage oath, dedicating you to a specific god or goddess. It is meant to be a dedication to Neo-Pagan Druidry as your primary path.

Of course, many people are on a dual path. They may be Wiccan and Druid, Druid and Discordian, or ADF and OBOD Druid. This is fine. The Dedicant Oath does not necessarily mean that you are choosing one over the other, but that Druidry is at least as important as your other path, if not more so.

ADF, your patrons, and your Grove are not the path of Neo-Pagan Druidry. They're simply vehicles that you use to travel it. Even after a person has finished the DP, they sometimes find that ADF is not for them. If you decide that ADF is not right for you and have made an Oath to follow ADF for the rest of your life, what will you do?

Similarly, patron deities are not always permanent. Some ADF members have been involved with a single deity their entire lives, but this is a rarity. Often, new patrons arrive, old ones depart, and sometimes many join the mix. Remember that you need to be open to new influences and new turns that may occur on your path.

To this end, think about how you express your Neo-Pagan Druidry, and think about how you might oath about that.

Homework:

In your Dedicant Notebook, write down the aspects about the Old Ways that appeal to you most. If you have encountered any sort of powers that aid you (certain nature spirits, deities, or ancestors), write them down. If you have taken a magical name (certainly not required) that you use to approach the spirits, write that down. If you have settled on a specific hearth culture, write that down.

If you have a dual path, write about how your other path interacts (or doesn't) with Neo-Pagan Druidry.

If you have a Patron (not everyone does), write about him or her (or them) and describe what you think they would like to see in your Oath. Consider how they want you to live your life, and how that reflects the virtues and commitments of Neo-Pagan Druidry.

Finally, it is good to write down what "Neo-Pagan Druidry" is to you, in your own words.

Writing these things down now will help you later when you go to write the final version of your Oath, and you might be surprised also to see how much things have changed.

Also, you should be nearly done with your Indo-European studies book. We will begin the next book in six weeks, so if you've been behind, start getting caught up!

Suggested Exercise: "The Inner Grove: Seeking a Tool"

Back in Week 8, then again in Week 14, we did exercises to locate and experience your Inner Grove. This week, we're going to travel out from that Grove to seek something once again: a tool for use on the journey we're taking.

Many paths lead outward from the center of our sacred Groves. This meditation will show you another of them. This meditation is available on the Three Cranes Grove, ADF, website, here: <http://threecranes.org/meditations/dpwoty/> This is the second meditation in this series, "The Inner Grove: Seeking a Tool," under the "Week 19" heading.

Week 20: The Nine Virtues: Vision

Related to Requirement: #1 – Nine Virtues

Required Reading:

- *Our Own Druidry*, p. 13 ("Virtue, Piety and Study" & "Nine Pagan Virtues");
- *Our Own Druidry*, p. 81-86 ("Lore and Essays")

Optional Reading:

- A Virtuous Life Nine Virtues study guide by Rev. Michael J Dangler: <https://www.adf.org/system/files/members/training/dp/publications/dp-req-1-nine-virtues.pdf>

Welcome to the third of the Nine Virtues, vision! Vision is, of course, the third in the first triad we explained in Week 13, the triad that corresponds to the priestly class. You might consider going back to read through Week 13's lesson to get a background if you have forgotten some of it.

Homework:

Our Own Druidry defines Vision as follows: "The ability to broaden one's perspective to have a greater understanding of our place/role in the cosmos, relating to the past, present, and future."

Read through that statement until you think you understand it. In your Dedicant Notebook, answer the following questions: Does that definition cover vision in your eyes? Is it simply seeing and understanding, or is there more to it?

What does the definition mean by "our place/role in the cosmos" and "past, present, and future"? Do these terms sit well with you?

If that definition doesn't quite sit right with you, head to your nearest dictionary and read the definitions in that it provides. Write it down (it is strongly recommended that you include a dictionary definition in your final write-up). Do any of those definitions make sense? Can they encompass all that vision is?

Now think of your own personal view of vision. Try to write it down in words. Feel free to steal phrases from the dictionary or the Handbook if you need to. Can you come up with a definition of vision that makes good sense to you?

Now, think about people you know whom you would call "visionary". Examine why you think of them that way: is it something they know, something they do, or something they have said? Is it something beyond this? Can you find words to describe it?

Does vision go beyond simply seeing? Does it involve seeing outside and inside? What does the DP Handbook mean when it talks about "relating to the past, present, and future"? Is it talking about divination, or merely seeing the outcome of traveling certain paths?

Think about myths and legends from different cultures. How was vision shown in the myths and legends? Was there a character in a myth that showed real vision? How was that vision displayed (in the *Volsungasaga*, Brynhild pronounces visions of the future; how does this fit with your idea of vision)?

Do you see yourself as visionary? Visionary in some ways but not others, perhaps? Not visionary at all? Does one need to be visionary to understand the concept of vision, or to wonder if something is visionary? Can anyone have vision?

Think of a time when you have exemplified this virtue. How did you feel? Did you know that this was a virtue at the time? Now think about a time when you failed to show this virtue. How did that make you feel? Did you feel as if you'd done something wrong or inadequate?

Finally, is vision a Virtue? Is it one that you agree should be on ADF's list? Why was it chosen? What is it about vision that either makes it a Virtue or keeps it from being one? If you have decided that it is not a Virtue, would you suggest another term, removing it altogether, or replacing it with something else entirely?

Now, go back through your answers to these questions and form a response of at least 125 words to "describe your understanding of the Virtue of vision."

And you have your third virtues essay out of the way!

Week 21: Nature Awareness 2

Related to Requirement: #7 – Nature Awareness

Required Reading:

- _Our Own Druidry_, p. 39 – 43 ("Attunement to Nature and the Kindred")

Suggested Reading:

- "Connecting With the Natural World" by Ladytoad <http://www.adf.org/rituals/meditations/connecting-with-the-natural-world.html>;
- "On the Solitary Path" by Ladytoad <http://www.adf.org/articles/solitary/ol-15.html>;
- "O Earth Mother, We Praise Thee" from _The Druid Chronicles_ <http://www.adf.org/articles/nature/oh-earth-mother.html>;
- _Sacred Fire, Holy Well_ by Ian Corrigan, p. 285 – 299 ("Concerning the Noble Clans" & "Conjuring the Sidhe");
- _The Solitary Druid_ by Rev. Skip Ellison, p. 60 – 73 ("Contacting the Land" to the end of that chapter)

You have been visiting your own special natural space for 18 weeks now, and by now you should have a strong connection to the space. If you don't yet, don't worry. Simply continue working in the spot. A connectedness to nature is not grown overnight, and it might take a long time to reach a level where you do feel truly connected.

As this connection forms, though, you can use it to branch out and become aware of nature and interconnectedness on a much larger scale. To do this, you will need to combine the practical experience of nature with knowledge of your place within it.

The homework questions will help you gain some of this knowledge (and, as a special bonus hint, it might also help you if you decide to move onto a further study program, too, so keep it available!)

Homework:

In your Dedicant Notebook, answer the following questions:

1. Where does your trash go?
2. Are there options for recycling that you're making use of? Why or why not?
3. Are there steps you can take to help reduce the amount of refuse you create?
4. What happens to your wastewater?
5. What rivers are nearby? Do you have a connection to them? What sort of connection?
6. Describe the basic climate of your area. Is it often wet and rainy? Dry and sunny? Wet and sunny? How has this affected the kinds of plants and animals in the area?
7. What visible effects have humans had on the natural landscapes around you?
8. Where do the winds usually come from? Are there different winds at different times of the year?

9. What major crops are grown in your region? Why are these particular crops grown here?
10. Where does your power come from (i.e. nuclear, solar, coal, gas, etc.)?

You may not be able to answer all these questions today, but as you answer them, you should begin to see how your life in particular is affected by the way humans interact with nature, and in seeing that, you will hopefully be able to see your own place within the web of nature.

Write a short paragraph about where you are now, and one about where you would like to be.

Week 22: The Fourth High Holy Day: An Explanation

Related to Requirement: #2 – Meaning and Discussion of High Days

Required Reading:

- *Our Own Druidry*, p. 60 – 72 ("Hearth Cultures & High Days")
- *ADF Constitution*, Article 4
- *The ADF Core Order of Ritual for High Days*,
  <http://www.adf.org/rituals/explanations/core-order.html>

Optional Reading:

- *Our Own Druidry*, p. 49 – 73 (The Very Basics of Ritual);
- *Appendix 1: Resources and Rituals for the Wheel of the Year* in this book;
- Step by Step through a Druid Worship Ceremony,
  <http://www.adf.org/rituals/explanations/stepbystep.html>;
- The "Liturgy and Rituals" section of the ADF page,
  <http://www.adf.org/rituals/>
- The Three Cranes Grove, ADF, outline of ritual (with example prayers),
  <http://www.threecranes.org/liturgy/>
- *The Crane Breviary and Guide Book* from the Order of the Crane:
  <https://www.adf.org/system/files/members/orders/crane/print/cbgb-preview.pdf>
- Rev. Skip Ellison's *The Solitary Druid*, appropriate high day in Chapters 6 & 7
- Nicholas Egelhoff's *Sunna's Journey: Norse Liturgy Through the Wheel of the Year*, appropriate High Day description

Welcome to your fourth High Holy Day as an ADF Dedicant. Next week's lesson will be a recap of the rite you do for this holiday

If your culture does not celebrate a specific feast, remember that most cultures had a festival or feast that would have been similar in intent and form, but it may have been celebrated at a different time of year. Unfortunately, much of the work of discovering which festival might match up to which High Day must be left to the individual Dedicant. Your mentor, of course is available for some help, but we urge you to seek out one of the culture-specific email lists to ask questions on. Quite often, they will be of more help than your mentor can be.

The eight High Days are outlined on pages 60 – 72 of *Our Own Druidry*. If you are not of a Celtic hearth culture or you simply wish to expand your horizons and try a different culture because you are unsure what to do, locate a feast that seems appropriate, where it gives a short description of the feast. Take that description and work to find a compatible feast in your hearth culture for that particular High Day.

A lot of the High Holy Days are obviously agrarian-based. If the High Day feels "irrelevant," seek our relevance. Can you find the rhythms of nature in the city? Look hard for them, and I'll bet you can find something fresh and new in your climate that corresponds with this season.

Homework:

Now, in your Dedicant Notebook, reflect on this High Holy Day. Consider how it is celebrated in your hearth culture, or across hearth cultures. Are there any myths that are celebrated in connection with this feast? If so, what are they, and how do they fit in? What does this holiday or time of year mean to you? Do you look forward to it? Are there secular aspects of the holiday that mean a lot to you, or perhaps holdovers or memories of your childhood that you cherish? How do you know when this day arrives? Do you look at the calendar, or do you just *know* it has come? If you have children (or wish to have children), what key traditions do you wish to pass down to them? What, if anything, is spiritual or religious to you about this High Day or time of year, and how do you show that? Are there any traditions that your Grove has for this High Day? Finally, is there anything else about this holiday that you would like to add?

There, you've just written another essay on a High Holy Day, and you're halfway through your training!

If you have a local Grove that you attend, then you should already have a rite you can attend. If you are solitary (and even if you do have a Grove, I still recommend), though, you will need to write and perform your own ritual for this rite. Because only four High Days are required to be done as ADF rituals, you don't need to be too concerned with exactly how to do an ADF rite, but you should certainly have something written up, or else go to the ADF website and find a ritual that will fit your hearth culture and use that. We do not expect you to be a skilled liturgist this early in the journey. Make sure that you have a rite ready before you intend to do the ritual, though, because last minute ritual writing is never fun for anyone.

See Appendix 1 for more information on what the High Day is about, where we have provided a number of links to help you think about the High Days themselves (and included places to find some example rituals for you to work from!)

Also, continue visiting the spot that helps keep you connected to Nature. You might make notes in your Dedicant Notebook about what you see, or if there are animals that appear often or plants that strike you as intriguing or odd. Make sure that you also record any experiences of power or sudden flashes of insight that you might have.

Finally, write about your fourteenth week of meditation: experiences, breath pattern, difficulties. . . all these things are good to write down.

Week 23: Fourth High Day Recap

Related to Requirement: #8 – High Days Attended
Required Reading: None.

You've made it through your fourth ritual, which means you're half-way through the wheel of the year with your Dedicant studies! Congratulations! It's now time to add to your essays for the Dedicant Path documentation by writing a recap of the rite!

Homework:

First, we've provided a sort of ritual write-up template that will help you get all the commonly needed details down in Appendix 2. You cannot just turn in a number of those sheets and expect to pass this requirement, though: you need to be much more in-depth. So grab some paper and start thinking about the rite by asking some good questions.

Let's start out with an easy one: how did the rite go in terms of structure? What things went wrong during the ritual? What things went right? Who were the patrons of the rite, and who was the gatekeeper? Did you have problems with saying the words without stumbling, or did everything come out smoothly? Did you forget to bring a sacrifice? Were you alone, or with a group? If you were with a group, did you say anything or do anything? Now, for the not so easy part: how did the rite go in terms of function and feeling? Did you feel anything during the ritual? Did you experience doubt or confidence? Can you describe what happened? If you were with a group, what did the other people say about what happened? What omens were drawn (if any), and what did they tell you? Could you feel the presence of any deities, spirits, or powers? What else about the rite struck you, or do you want to share?

If you answer those questions, you've just finished another essay for the Dedicant Path documentation!

Also, make sure you're still visiting your natural space, and taking notes as you go. The notes will help greatly when you go to write your final essay on Nature Awareness.

Week 24: The Two Powers

Related to Requirement: #5 – Two Powers
Suggested Reading:
- "An Advanced Two Powers Attunement" by Linda Demissy
  <http://www.adf.org/rituals/meditations/advanced-two-powers.html>
- Ian Corrigan, "Working Magic with the Two Powers",
  <https://www.adf.org/articles/working/two-powers-magic.html>
- "The Two Powers: an Alternative for Large Rites" by Rev. Kirk Thomas
  <http://www.adf.org/rituals/meditations/two-powers-group.html>
- "Bungee Cord Two Powers" by Bert Kelher,
  <http://www.adf.org/members/training/dp/articles/bungee-2powers.html>
- "Two Powers on a String and a Prayer" by Anne Lenzi,
  <http://www.adf.org/members/training/dp/articles/2p-string-prayer.html>
- *Sacred Fire, Holy Well* by Ian Corrigan, p. 78 – 80 ("Three Druidic Hallows" &
  "Ritual Traditions of Fire and Water"); p. 226 – 235 ("Three Cauldron Spells"
  & "Brigid's Fire and Water")
- *The Fire on Our Hearth* by Three Cranes Grove, ADF, p. 156 – 158 ("Two
  Powers – Convection," "Two Powers – Crocus Meditation," "Book
  Attunement")

Suggested Audio
- Rev. Jenni Hunt's "Two Powers Crocus" meditation:
  <http://threecranes.org/media/JHunt-MJD-crocus-meditation.mp3>
- Rev. Michael J Dangler's "Nine Breaths" meditation:
  <http://threecranes.org/media/mjd-nine-breaths.mp3>
- Rev. Michael J Dangler's "Inner Gates" meditation:
  <http://threecranes.org/media/MJD-Inner-Gates-Meditation.mp3>

Hopefully, at this point you have been doing the Two Powers meditation with some regularity. We also hope you have had some success with these Two Powers or Two Currents, and you should have a good idea about how they interact from a purely experiential point of view.

As mentioned in our last Two Powers section, there are prayers and chants that help explain the cosmos of ritual. Here is a chant by a Three Cranes Grove, ADF, member:

Transpiration/Inspiration
By Shawneen

Take it up
Let it go
Within us now
Begin to flow

Call it down
We knit the round
Within us know
We need to grow

Shawneen also says of the above: "I have been using a few stanzas of it as my two powers meditation/trance induction in my own personal devotions. I find drawing out the last word of each line creates a nice sonorous song line. Give it a try! Enjoy!"

Homework:

You've been working with the Two powers meditation for 13 weeks now. How has this meditation felt to you? Do you do this meditation as your daily meditation, or as part of daily rituals? Can you describe how it feels?

What parts of the meditation move you the most? The least? Does one power or the other seem stronger?

Many people will come to feel that one of these powers is masculine and one is feminine. In your Dedicant Notebook, write a short paragraph on how the Sky Power is masculine and the Earth Power is feminine. Now, write another short paragraph about how the Sky Power is feminine and the Earth Power is masculine. Can you make both arguments? Which one convinces you more? Is either worth arguing?

The Sky Power is sometimes described as "ordering" and the Earth Power is sometimes described as "chaotic". Do you feel this is an accurate description of the Powers?

If you have chosen a hearth culture, how does the mythology of that culture embrace the Two Powers?

Can you write a chant or a prayer about the way the cosmos looks when we're in ritual? Try writing one and using it as a meditation aid, and write down your results.

Two Powers

Week 25: The Nine Virtues: Courage

Related to Requirement: #1 – Nine Virtues
Required Reading:

- *Our Own Druidry*, p. 13 ("Virtue, Piety and Study" & "Nine Pagan Virtues");
- *Our Own Druidry*, p. 81-86 ("Lore and Essays")

Optional Reading:

- "Warrior Virtues" by Paul Maurice
  <http://www.adf.org/members/guilds/warriors/ethics-virtues.html>;
- A Virtuous Life Nine Virtues study guide by Rev. Michael J Dangler:
  <https://www.adf.org/system/files/members/training/dp/publications/dp-req-1-nine-virtues.pdf>;
- *Oak Leaves* issue #14, "Ethics of a Celtic Warrior" by Robert Barton

Welcome to the fourth of the Nine Virtues, courage! Courage is, of course, the first in the second triad I explained in week 13, the triad that corresponds to the warrior class. You might consider going back to read through Week 13's lesson to get a background if you have forgotten some of it.

Homework:

Our Own Druidry defines Courage as follows: "The ability to act appropriately in the face of danger."

Read through that statement until you think you understand it. In your Dedicant Notebook, answer the following questions: Does that definition cover courage in your eyes? Is it simply bravery and action, or is there more to it?

What does the definition mean by "act appropriately" and "the face of danger"? Do these terms sit well with you? Are they too vague, or perhaps too specific?

If that definition doesn't quite sit right with you, head to your nearest dictionary and read the definitions in that it provides. Write it down (it is strongly recommended that you include a dictionary definition in your final write-up). Do any of those definitions make sense? Can they encompass all that courage is?

Now think of your own personal view of courage. Try to write it down in words. Feel free to steal phrases from the dictionary or the Handbook if you need to. Can you come up with a definition of courage that makes good sense to you?

Now, think about people you know whom you would call "courageous". Examine why you think of them that way: is it something they know, something they do or the way they did it, or something they have said? Is it something beyond this? Can you find words to describe it?

Does courage go beyond simply bravery? Does it involve decisiveness and strength? What does the DP Handbook mean when it talks about "acting appropriately?" Is it talking about doing something specific, or merely doing what is right at the time?

Think about myths and legends from different cultures. How was courage shown in the myths and legends? Was there a character in a myth that showed real courage? How was that courage displayed (in the *Odyssey*, Odysseus goes to the threshold of the Underworld; how does this fit with your idea of courage)?

Do you see yourself as courageous? Courageous in some ways but not others, perhaps? Not courageous at all? Does one need to be courageous to understand the concept of courage, or to wonder if something is courageous? Can anyone have courage?

Think of a time when you have exemplified this virtue. How did you feel? Did you know that this was a virtue at the time? Now think about a time when you failed to show this virtue. How did that make you feel? Did you feel as if you'd done something wrong or inadequate?

Are there lines from books, famous people, songs, or movies that particularly stick with you and illustrate this Virtue, such as the "Litany Against Fear" in *Dune* or Roosevelt's famous, "The only thing we have to fear is fear itself" line? How do these affect your conception of courage?

Finally, is courage a Virtue? Is it one that you agree should be on ADF's list? Why was it chosen? What is it about courage that either makes it a Virtue or keeps it from being one? If you have decided that it is not a Virtue, would you suggest another term, removing it altogether, or replacing it with something else entirely?

Now, go back through your answers to these questions and form a response of at least 125 words to "describe your understanding of the Virtue of courage."

And you have your fourth virtues essay out of the way!

Keep in mind, **your first book report is due next week**: finish it up if you haven't already!

Week 26: Second Book Started: Modern Paganism

Related to Requirement: #3 – Book Reviews

Required Reading:

- *Our Own Druidry*, p. 17 – 18 ("Concerning the Reading of Books")
- *Our Own Druidry*, Appendix B, p. xii – xiii ("Writing a book review")
- start on one book from the list of Pagan Revival titles at the ADF Website, <u>A Recommended Reading List</u>: <<u>https://www.adf.org/training/resources/reading.html</u>>

One of the reasons many people come to ADF is because they are looking for a religion or organization that is interested in both piety and study. Because this is a rare combination in the Neo-Pagan community, we are very proud to offer such things. We do expect our Dedicants to be well-versed in the basic scholarship behind ADF, the modern Neo-Pagan movement, and the historical roots of Neo-Paganism in general.

To this end, three book reviews are asked of all Dedicants, one in Indo-European studies (because ADF is an Indo-European based organization), one general Neo-Pagan movement book (because we are Neo-Pagan), and one book on one of the Indo-European hearth cultures (generally the hearth culture that the Dedicant will choose to work with).

We will work on the Modern Paganism title as your next book. The main idea is to help you understand where Neo-Paganism has been, because you will become part of where it is going through your work in ADF.

As we do not expect you to finish the book you choose in one week, we will give you questions to think about now, and will remind you occasionally throughout the coming weeks to continue reading. The book review for this title will be due on week 39.

By this point, you should have written up your review for your IE studies book. If you have not, here is a refresher for what you should cover in the book review (and please keep them in mind as you begin this second book):

Remember to start all book reviews with the bibliographical information. What is the book about? Is there a main thesis? Can you summarize the main points? Why was this book on the reading list? Do you think it should be there? Does it inform your own personal practice in any way? Does it give you new ideas, crazy thoughts, or open your mind? Could you recommend this book to others? Do you have trouble understanding it, or is it a breeze? Are there things that would make it better?

Making an outline or notes as you read will be invaluable to writing your book review later.

Keep these questions in mind as you read through the book, and let your mentor know what you're reading so he or she can help answer any questions you might have!

Also, continue visiting the spot that helps keep you connected to Nature. You might make notes in your Dedicant Notebook about what you see, or if there are animals that appear often or plants that strike you as intriguing or odd.

Finally, continue to meditate and record your meditations thoroughly.

Week 27: The Nine Virtues: Integrity

Related to Requirement: #1 – Nine Virtues
Required Reading:
- *Our Own Druidry*, p. 13 ("Virtue, Piety and Study" & "Nine Pagan Virtues");
- *Our Own Druidry*, p. 81-86 ("Lore and Essays")

Optional Reading:
- "Warrior Virtues" by Paul Maurice <http://www.adf.org/members/guilds/warriors/ethics-virtues.html>;
- A Virtuous Life Nine Virtues study guide by Rev. Michael J Dangler: <https://www.adf.org/system/files/members/training/dp/publications/dp-req-1-nine-virtues.pdf>;
- *Oak Leaves* issue #14, "Ethics of a Celtic Warrior" by Robert Barton

Welcome to the fifth of the Nine Virtues, integrity! Integrity is, of course, the second in the second triad I explained in week 13, the triad that corresponds to the warrior class. You might consider going back to read through Week 13's lesson to get a background if you have forgotten some of it.

Homework:

Our Own Druidry defines integrity as follows: "Honor; being trustworthy to oneself and to others, involving oath-keeping, honesty, fairness, respect, self-confidence."

Read through that statement until you think you understand it. In your Dedicant Notebook, answer the following questions: Does that definition cover integrity in your eyes? Is it simply keeping your word and being honest, or is there more to it?

What does the definition mean by "oath-keeping" and "self-confidence"? Do these terms sit well with you? Are they too vague, or perhaps too specific?

If that definition doesn't quite sit right with you, head to your nearest dictionary and read the definitions in that it provides. Write it down (it is strongly recommended that you include a dictionary definition in your final write-up). Do any of those definitions make sense? Can they encompass all that integrity is?

Now think of your own personal view of integrity. Try to write it down in words. Feel free to steal phrases from the dictionary or the Handbook if you need to. Can you come up with a definition of integrity that makes good sense to you?

Now, think about people you know who has what you would call "integrity". Examine why you think of them that way: is it something they know, something they do or the way they did it, or something they have said? Is it something beyond this? Can you find words to describe it?

Does integrity go beyond simply keeping your word? Does it involve fair judgment and respect? What does the DP Handbook mean when it talks about having "self-confidence"? Is it talking about doing something specific, or merely being right by yourself at the time?

Think about other definitions of integrity, like the integrity of a structure, or the integrity of an argument. "Integrity" means something different here. Does this meaning help build your conception of integrity? Can it apply to you?

Think about myths and legends from different cultures. How was integrity shown in the myths and legends? Was there a character in a myth that showed real integrity? How was that integrity displayed (in the *Theogany*, Eris, the goddess of strife and discord, is listed as the mother of Oath; how does this fit with your idea of integrity)?

Do you see yourself as having integrity? Having integrity in some ways but not others, perhaps? Not having integrity at all? Does one need to have integrity to understand the concept of integrity, or to wonder if something is done with integrity? Can anyone have integrity?

Think of a time when you have exemplified this virtue. How did you feel? Did you know that this was a virtue at the time? Now think about a time when you failed to show this virtue. How did that make you feel? Did you feel as if you'd done something wrong or inadequate?

Finally, is integrity a Virtue? Is it one that you agree should be on ADF's list? Why was it chosen? What is it about integrity that either makes it a Virtue or keeps it from being one? If you have decided that it is not a Virtue, would you suggest another term, removing it altogether, or replacing it with something else entirely?

Now, go back through your answers to these questions and form a response of at least 125 words to "describe your understanding of the Virtue of integrity."

And you have your fifth virtues essay out of the way!

Week 28: The Fifth High Holy Day: An Explanation

Related to Requirement: #2 – Meaning and Discussion of High Days
Required Reading:
- *Our Own Druidry*, p. 60 – 72 (Hearth Cultures & High Days)
- *ADF Constitution*, Article 4
- *The ADF Core Order of Ritual for High Days*,
  <http://www.adf.org/rituals/explanations/core-order.html>

Optional Reading:
- *Our Own Druidry*, p. 49 – 73 (The Very Basics of Ritual);
- *Appendix 1: Resources and Rituals for the Wheel of the Year* in this book;
- Step by Step through a Druid Worship Ceremony,
  <http://www.adf.org/rituals/explanations/stepbystep.html>;
- The "Liturgy and Rituals" section of the ADF page,
  <http://www.adf.org/rituals/>
- The Three Cranes Grove, ADF, outline of ritual (with example prayers),
  <http://www.threecranes.org/liturgy/>
- *The Crane Breviary and Guide Book* from the Order of the Crane:
  <https://www.adf.org/system/files/members/orders/crane/print/cbgb-preview.pdf>
- Rev. Skip Ellison's *The Solitary Druid*, appropriate high day in Chapters 6 & 7
- Nicholas Egelhoff's *Sunna's Journey: Norse Liturgy Through the Wheel of the Year*, appropriate High Day description

Welcome to your fifth High Holy Day as an ADF Dedicant. Next week's lesson will be a recap of the rite you do for this holiday.

If your culture does not celebrate a specific feast, remember that most cultures had a festival or feast that would have been similar in intent and form, but it may have been celebrated at a different time of year. Unfortunately, much of the work of discovering which festival might match up to which High Day must be left to the individual Dedicant. Your mentor, of course is available for some help, but we urge you to seek out one of the culture-specific email lists to ask questions on. Quite often, they will be of more help than your mentor can be.

The eight High Days are outlined on pages 60 – 72 of *Our Own Druidry*. If you are not of a Celtic hearth culture or you simply wish to expand your horizons and try a different culture because you are unsure what to do, locate a ritual that seems appropriate, where it gives a short description of the feast. Take that description and work to find a compatible feast in your hearth culture for that particular High Day.

A lot of the High Holy Days are obviously agrarian-based. If the High Day feels "irrelevant," seek our relevance. Can you find the rhythms of nature in the city? Look hard for them, and I'll bet you can find something fresh and new in your climate that corresponds with this season.

Homework:

Now, in your Dedicant Notebook, reflect on this High Holy Day. Consider how it is celebrated in your hearth culture, or across hearth cultures. Are there any myths that are celebrated in connection with this feast? If so, what are they, and how do they fit in? What does this holiday or time of year mean to you? Do you look forward to it? Are there secular aspects of the holiday that mean a lot to you, or perhaps holdovers or memories of your childhood that you cherish? How do you know when this day arrives? Do you look at the calendar, or do you just *know* it has come? If you have children (or wish to have children), what key traditions do you wish to pass down to them? What, if anything, is spiritual or religious to you about this High Day or time of year, and how do you show that? Are there any traditions that your Grove has for this High Day? Finally, is there anything else about this holiday that you would like to add?

There, you've just written another essay on a High Holy Day, and you're on the downhill slope leading toward the end of this first year!

If you have a local Grove that you attend, then you should already have a rite you can attend. If you are solitary (and even if you do have a Grove, I still recommend), though, you will need to write and perform your own ritual for this rite. Because only four High Days are required to be done as ADF rituals, you don't need to be too concerned with exactly how to do an ADF rite, but you should certainly have something written up, or else go to the ADF website and find a ritual that will fit your hearth culture and use that. We do not expect you to be a skilled liturgist this early in the journey. Make sure that you have a rite ready before you intend to do the ritual, though, because last minute ritual writing is never fun for anyone.

See Appendix 1 for more information on what the High Day is about, where we have provided a number of links to help you think about the High Days themselves (and included places to find some example rituals for you to work from!)

Also, continue visiting the spot that helps keep you connected to Nature. You might make notes in your Dedicant Notebook about what you see, or if there are animals that appear often or plants that strike you as intriguing or odd. Make sure that you also record any experiences of power or sudden flashes of insight that you might have.

Finally, write about your twenty-second week of meditation: experiences, breath pattern, difficulties. . . all these things are good to write down. Only a few weeks left!

Week 29: Fifth High Day Recap

Related to Requirement: #8 – High Days Attended
Required Reading: None.

You've made it through your fifth ritual, which means you're beyond half way through the wheel of the year with your Dedicant studies! Congratulations! It's now time to add to your essays for the Dedicant Path documentation by writing a recap of the rite!

Homework:

First, we've provided a sort of ritual write-up template that will help you get all the commonly needed details down in Appendix 2. You cannot just turn in a number of those sheets and expect to pass this requirement, though: you need to be much more in-depth. So grab some paper and start thinking about the rite by asking some good questions.

Let's start out with an easy one: how did the rite go in terms of structure? What things went wrong during the ritual? What things went right? Who were the patrons of the rite, and who was the gatekeeper? Did you have problems with saying the words without stumbling, or did everything come out smoothly? Did you forget to bring a sacrifice? Were you alone, or with a group? If you were with a group, did you say anything or do anything? Now, for the not so easy part: how did the rite go in terms of function and feeling? Did you feel anything during the ritual? Did you experience doubt or confidence? Can you describe what happened? If you were with a group, what did the other people say about what happened? What omens were drawn (if any), and what did they tell you? Could you feel the presence of any deities, spirits, or powers? What else about the rite struck you, or do you want to share?

If you answer those questions, you've just finished another essay for the Dedicant Path documentation!

Also, make sure you're still visiting your natural space, and taking notes as you go. The notes will help greatly when you go to write your final essay on Nature Awareness.

Suggested Exercise: "The Inner Grove: Seeking an Ally"

Back in Weeks 8, 14, and 19, we did exercises to locate and experience your Inner Grove. This week, we're going to travel out from that Grove to seek something once again: an Ally among the Spirits who will help you on this journey.

Many paths lead outward from the center of our sacred Groves. This meditation will show you another of them. This meditation is available on the Three Cranes Grove, ADF, website, here: <http://threecranes.org/meditations/dpwoty/> This is the second meditation in this series, "The Inner Grove: Seeking an Ally," under the "Week 29" heading.

Week 30: The Two Powers: Final Essay

Related to Requirement: #5 – Two Powers; #6 – Mental Training

Until now, you've been doing work with the Two Powers in ritual, meditation, and on your own. At this point, you should have a fairly clear understanding of what you're doing, how it builds a cosmos, and have a strong experience of the Powers involved.

In light of that, this week your assignment will be to write the final essay on the Two Powers and finish one of the requirements.

Homework:

The Two Powers requirement reads like this:

"An essay focusing on the Dedicant's understanding of the meaning of the 'Two Powers' meditation or other form of 'grounding and centering', as used in meditation and ritual. This account should include impressions and insights that the Dedicant gained from practical experience. (300 word min)"

A few general points about this requirement:

1. You don't have to talk about the Two Powers to fulfill the requirement; however, because we're trying to get the best understanding possible of ADF's form of Druidry, your essay should reflect it, and that's what this book will guide you through.
2. Note that it asks for "understanding," "meaning" and "insights from personal experience."
3. It also requests that you talk about its use in both meditation *and* ritual.

So, let's start with a set of questions that will help you work through this essay. Returning to your notes from our previous visitations with this requirement may help.

Describe the Two Powers meditation. What are the Two Powers that this meditation is named after? What are the properties of these two currents? What sort of cosmic picture do they paint? Why can they also be referred to as the Two Currents?

Can you think of any cultural adaptations of this meditation? If you've chosen a hearth culture, can you find anything within that culture that would be like the Two Powers? How would they be described in the cosmic reality of your chosen culture?

What binary systems are represented in the Two Powers? Chaos and Order? Light and Dark? Cold and Hot? Creative and Frozen? Goddess and God? Life and Death? Finally, are these really binary systems, or are they something else?

Do you find that one is masculine and one is feminine? Why do you feel this way? We did an exercise in Week 24 regarding the "gender" of the Powers: what experiences did you have with that?

Why do we use this form of grounding and centering in ritual? Why not another kind? Is there something in the cosmology that makes this particular form of centering ideal for ADF rites?

When you first did the Two Powers meditation, what happened? Did it go well? Were you able to see the visualizations? Did you have trouble with certain aspects of the meditation? Have these troubles increased or gone away?

Finally, as you have worked with the Two Powers meditation, have you changed anything to make the meditation fit your practice better? Does it work well as it is?

Congratulations, you've just finished your Two Powers Essay!

For one final bit of homework, make sure that you pay special attention to the natural space that you've been frequenting, because we'll be working with the Nature Spirits next week.

Week 31: The Three Kindred: Nature Spirits

Related to Requirement: #7 – Nature Awareness; #9 – Relationships to Kindred; #10 – Personal Religion

Required reading:
- *Our Own Druidry*, p. 26 ("The Nature Spirits");
- *Our Own Druidry*, p. 42 – 43 ("The Noble Spirits")

Suggested Reading:
- "Domovoy" by Katherine Milechkine <http://www.adf.org/articles/gods-and-spirits/slavic/domovoy.html>;
- "Local Nature Spirits," by Medb Aodhamair, <http://www.adf.org/articles/nature/local-nature-spirits.html>;
- "Why Icelanders are wary of elves living beneath the rocks," BBC magazine <http://www.bbc.com/news/magazine-27907358> & "Iceland's hidden elves delay road projects," NBC News <http://www.nbcnews.com/news/other/icelands-hidden-elves-delay-road-projects-f2D11792552>
- *The Solitary Druid* by Rev. Skip Ellison, p. 69 – 72 ("Spirits of Place")

Since Week Five, you've been visiting a place (or places) where you have worked to build an awareness of the natural world around you. At Week 23, we talked some more about your place in nature and how you can work with nature and the world around you. In Week 41, you will be asked to write your final essay about nature awareness for the DP, and so it's about time we started talking about the spirits of place around you.

The second of the Three Kindred are the Nature Spirits. Often called the Noble Ones, Land Wights, or the Sidhe (pronounced "She"), these are the elves and faeries and trolls and gnomes who have earned a prominent place in Neo-Paganism. They are also our animal guides and our household spirits, and we turn to them to keep our worlds in order and to give them honor for their continuance of the cycles of nature.

There are even modern-day examples of Nature Spirits being remembered in various Indo-European countries. In Iceland, for example, roads are built around elf-homes, rather than over them. To this day, there are actually people who are called in to make sure that none of these homes are disturbed.[4]

Many times, you will hear people tell about how the Naturekin like small, shiny objects or ribbons as offerings. They also like to be left milk and honey, or a portion of your meals as an offering. If you have a home spirit, you might want to leave them regular offerings, because they have a tendency to wreak havoc if you do not maintain a relationship of reciprocity.

The spirits of place have always been there and always will be there. They are part of the cycles of nature, and remembering them is very important if you want to live in this world. A good relationship with the Noble Ones will bring you luck and protection when you need it,

---

[4] http://www.nytimes.com/2005/07/13/international/europe/13elves.html

and part of that good relationship involves helping to keep your relationship with the natural world intact.

Homework:

Think about how you work with Nature Spirits: do you work with specific spirits? Do you have animal guides? Write down who they are and what they do for you, and then write down what you do for them. What sort of relationship is it?

How do you remember and honor these spirits? Do you leave them offerings, or do work that protects their homes and lives? Do you simply connect? What is the nature of your connection with these spirits? Write these things down in your Dedicant Notebook for future reference.

Remember to keep visiting your site for observing nature. Think about changes in the seasons since you started. Are there landscape changes? Do you feel a connection to the land? Now that we've talked about Nature Spirits, do you have interactions with them? Write these in your Dedicant Notebook for reference, also.

Week 32: Meditation Reflection and Final Essay

Related to Requirement: #6 – Mental Training; #10 – Personal Religion

At this point, the meditation you began in week 7 has been going on for five months, which is the minimum you are asked to do for the Dedicant Path documentation. This week, we will look at your notes from the past 26 weeks, and piece them together in an essay for submission.

On a side note, this requirement is the one that trips the most Dedicants up, mainly because they can't continue meditating for 26 weeks. If you've gotten this far and meditated at least once per week, you're well ahead of the game.

If you have not finished the meditation, simply continue to meditate. At this point, we're only part-way through the year, so there's no rush. But I would encourage you to meditate as much as possible and to write it down as often as possible. Save this lesson until you have 26 *straight* weeks of meditation.

Homework:

Let's start with the requirement:

"6. An essay or journal covering the Dedicant's personal experience of building mental discipline, through the use of meditation, trance, or other systematic techniques on a regular basis. The experiences in the essay or journal should cover at least a five month period. (800 words min.)"

This requirement asks for a few things. First, it requests that whatever you turn in include your "personal experience" in "building mental discipline" using some sort of "systematic" technique on a "regular basis."

Wow, that's a lot. What's it all mean?

According to the requirement, as it's listed above, you can simply turn in your meditation journal and be done with it. It must be pointed out, though, that you will not gain as much from the journal as you would from an essay that reviews and analyzes the meditation you have done. Because of this, we greatly prefer to receive a reflective essay, and we hope that you will prefer this as well. There is also the issue of many Dedicants not wanting to turn in their meditation journals because they include private thoughts. To that end, I will list a general set of things to cover and think about in your essay. Make sure you get out your journal, though, because you can't write this essay without it.

That said, to begin with, you need to discuss what you were doing from a generally objective perspective, and you need to show that what you did was "systematic" and "regular."

Begin by talking about what you started out doing. Did you use a breath count? Where did you meditate? Did you create a meditation seat? What techniques did you try, and how long did you try them for? If you failed at something, how long did you work at it before either it worked, or you gave up? If you settled into one technique toward the end, what was it? Please be as specific as possible when describing your techniques. Remember, you're looking to show that your meditation was "systematic," not "erratic."

As for "regular," if you write down all the dates you did the meditation exercises and average them up, how many times per week were you meditating? Or is it more appropriate to ask how many times *per day*? The more the better, of course, but if it was only a couple times a week on average, remember that everyone meditates at a different rate.

The requirement also asks that you show "personal experience." One of the advantages that the essay has over just turning in your journal entries is that you can hold back some of your more private and personal experiences. Meditation is an intensely personal experience, and sometimes we do not wish to share every detail. Still, to complete this requirement, some personal experience will need to be shown. Remember, we're not asking for all the details you have; rather, we're asking for a level of detail that shows that you worked hard at this and that your experiences with this have aided you in your spiritual growth. In the essay, you might quote or intersperse the essay with journal entries (or parts of them) to show this personal experience.

The essay must also show that you have "built mental discipline." This doesn't mean that you've managed to lift things with your mind. It means that you've come to an understanding of how to quiet your mind and think clearly, how to use the skill of opening to nature in ritual, or how to see with greater clarity into the Otherworld. In the end, it doesn't matter so much what mental discipline you build (it may simply be the ability to sit for an hour each day and be bored yet quiet), but it does matter that you build it.

Kind of going along with the "building of mental discipline" bit, you might talk about plans to continue your meditation journal, or to work with new and interesting ways of meditation that you haven't tried yet.

Finally, if you have been working your tail off, trying to find some way to make meditation "work" and you feel you've failed miserably, tell us that! Meditation isn't for everyone. It may not work for you at all. This could be for any number of reasons: the techniques that you try don't work for your brain; you can't meditate indoors and haven't tried it outdoors yet; or you're just too fidgety to sit still for an hour. Whatever the cause, the important thing will be that you have tried, and done your best to finish this requirement. Some of the best essays are from people who never managed to meditate, but had a lot of fun trying.

Finish an essay on that (and cover those three things), and you're done with the meditation requirement!

We do suggest you continue working with meditation. Remember: this requirement was meant to help you grasp key concepts in ADF Druidry: the Silence, being open to nature, etc. If you don't quite have them down (and very few people do at five months), keep working!

Week 33: The Nine Virtues: Perseverance

Related to Requirement: #1 – Nine Virtues
Required Reading:

- *Our Own Druidry*, p. 13 ("Virtue, Piety and Study" & "Nine Pagan Virtues");
- *Our Own Druidry*, p. 81-86 ("Lore and Essays")

Optional Reading:

- "Sacred Work, Sacred Life" by Judith Anderson Morris (Ladytoad) <http://www.adf.org/articles/identity/sacred-work-sacred-life.html>
- "Warrior Virtues" by Paul Maurice <http://www.adf.org/members/guilds/warriors/ethics-virtues.html>;
- A Virtuous Life Nine Virtues study guide by Rev. Michael J Dangler: <https://www.adf.org/system/files/members/training/dp/publications/dp-req-1-nine-virtues.pdf>;
- *Oak Leaves* issue #14, "Ethics of a Celtic Warrior" by Robert Barton
- The Man Who Planted Trees by Jean Giono <http://home.infomaniak.ch/arboretum/Man_Tree.htm>

Welcome to the sixth of the Nine Virtues, perseverance! Perseverance is, of course, the third in the second triad I explained in week 13, the triad that corresponds to the warrior class. You might consider going back to read through Week 13's lesson to get a background if you have forgotten some of it.

Homework:

Our Own Druidry defines perseverance as follows: "Drive; the motivation to pursue goals even when that pursuit becomes difficult."

Read through that statement until you think you understand it. In your Dedicant Notebook, answer the following questions: Does that definition cover perseverance in your eyes? Is it simply persistence, or is there more to it?

What does the definition mean by "drive" and "motivation"? Do these terms sit well with you? Are they too vague, or perhaps too specific?

If that definition doesn't quite sit right with you, head to your nearest dictionary and read the definitions in that it provides. Write it down (it is strongly recommended that you include a dictionary definition in your final write-up). Do any of those definitions make sense? Can they encompass all that perseverance is?

Now think of your own personal view of perseverance. Try to write it down in words. Feel free to steal phrases from the dictionary or the Handbook if you need to. Can you come up with a definition of perseverance that makes good sense to you?

Now, think about people you know whom you would say have "persevered". Examine why you think of them that way: is it something they know, something they do or the way they did it, or something they have said? Is it something beyond this? Can you find words to describe it?

Does perseverance go beyond simply completing tasks? Does it involve decisiveness and the timely finishing of tasks? What does the DP Handbook mean when it talks about "motivation"? Is it talking about doing something specific, or merely getting things done?

Think about myths and legends from different cultures. How was perseverance shown in the myths and legends? Was there a character in a myth that showed real perseverance? How was that perseverance displayed (in the Odyssey, Odysseus sails for ten years before finally coming home and meeting the challenges there; how does this fit with your idea of perseverance)?

Do you see yourself as persevering? Persevering in some ways but not others, perhaps? Not persevering at all? Does one need to persevere consistently to understand the concept of perseverance, or to wonder about perseverance? Can anyone have perseverance?

Think of a time when you have exemplified this virtue. How did you feel? Did you know that this was a virtue at the time? Now think about a time when you failed to show this virtue. How did that make you feel? Did you feel as if you'd done something wrong or inadequate?

Finally, is perseverance a Virtue? Is it one that you agree should be on ADF's list? Why was it chosen? What is it about perseverance that either makes it a Virtue or keeps it from being one? If you have decided that it is not a Virtue, would you suggest another term, removing it altogether, or replacing it with something else entirely?

Now, go back through your answers to these questions and form a response of at least 125 words to "describe your understanding of the Virtue of perseverance."

And you have your sixth virtues essay out of the way!

Week 34: Personal Religion

Related to Requirement: #10 – Personal Religion; #9 – Relationships to Kindred
Required Reading:

- *Our Own Druidry*, p. 17 ("The Hearth Oath")
- *Our Own Druidry*, p. 117 – 122 ("Personalizing Your Paganism")
- *Our Own Druidry*, p. xv – xvi ("Appendix 1: Adapting the DP to Specific Ethnic Paths")

Optional reading:

- *Sacred Fire, Holy Well* by Ian Corrigan, p. 264 – 267 ("The Waiting Shrine") & p. 277 – 279 ("Working With the Patron")
- *Sacred Gifts* by Kirk Thomas, p. 182 – 201 ("Two Simple Rituals of Connection")

At this point, well over half-way into a year of Dedicant work, you will probably have seen many people who have chosen a hearth culture, talk about Patron deities, and are very specific in their knowledge of their culture. Most often, people become interested in a specific culture, and then interested in ADF, and they might start by looking at their hearth culture.

In the end, it's personal choice. It's your religion. You will do with it as you please, and you might just take your time getting there. It's a fun ride, so enjoy it!

A word about Patrons: Once upon a time, there was a Patron Oath requirement in the old Dedicant Path. It was removed in the 2003 revisions because the Clergy Council (and a large number of members) felt that a one-year study program was not nearly enough time for someone to find and build a relationship with a Patron. We know that each person is individual and will find a Patron at their own rate. Some people are hit full in the face with a Patron within minutes of deciding that they have become Pagan, while others are Pagan for years (even decades!) before finding any trace of a Patron. Sometimes, a Patron will not be around for someone's entire life, but will show up and fade away quickly.

The relationship between the human and the Patron is not one of parity. While the relationship is still reciprocal, it is far more giving on the side of the Patron. The Patron has things that we cannot hope to obtain ourselves (generally, "blessings"), and we know this. Rather than attempt a purely 1:1 relationship on gifts, the Patron is there to provide us with what we need, generally asking only what we are able to provide in return. It is a benevolent relationship, and the power (not always a deity, but usually) is giving of his/her own good will to you.

This does not make the relationship one of *taketaketake*, but rather of giving what cannot be obtained any other way, and asking for something of lesser value in return. These are special relationships built on love and on charity, and should never be taken for granted.

A final note about personal religion: it's just that: personal. ADF is all about Indo-European culture, deities, and ritual, but that doesn't mean that we require our members to be the same. If you want to worship non-IE deities and pantheons (such as Hindu, Egyptian, Tibetan, or Native American powers), that's up to you, and ADF will never ask you to give up those personal beliefs. On the other hand, public rites that are billed as "ADF Rituals" do need to be IE in focus, though other aspects might be added in (for instance, honoring the Native Americans whose bones lie in the land, who made this land sacred before we arrived, would be appropriate). While your main practice should be within the confines of IE religion, we know that you may have ties to other cultural/religious groups, or even to patrons who are not of the Indo-European family. Feel free to elaborate on those aspects in your essays on personal religion: if they are important to you, they are important to us.

Homework:

In your Dedicant Notebook, write a bit about what interests you in various hearth cultures. If you're already settled on a hearth culture, skip to the next paragraph. What sort of things are you looking for in a culture? Do you have an ancestral tie to a certain culture, or is this even important to you? Are there myths that you find a commonality with? Are there cultural aspects that you particularly like? When the topic of cultures comes up, do certain ones stand out to you? In week 40, we will choose a book on a specific culture for you to read. Remember that when you choose that book, you are not tied to that culture for worship, or to use as a hearth culture. Consider it exploration.

To make matters more complicated, often in IE societies there is more than one set of Gods. This is most noticeable in Norse, where you have the Vanir and the Aesir. Does one set of gods speak out more to you than the other? What can you find out about them? Do you find an affinity to the attributes of a set of gods?

Now, let's get really complicated and talk about Patrons. If you're really gung-ho about Patronage, though, you'll want to start by looking into the myths and symbols that appeal to you. Do certain things show up over and over again? Are there aspects of your personal life that you need help with? Are there deities who intrigue you, amuse you, or frighten you? Is there a Goddess who affects a large part of your life? If you're answering with the same deity over and over, you might just have a Patron. If not, give it time.

And always examine the relationship carefully!

Now, what happens if you're drawn to two different pantheons? Or, worse, to a Patron who isn't in the pantheon you chose? Have no fear: it's remarkably common in ADF. Each person deals with it in their own way, so a lot of it is up to you to work out. You can, though, ask around and find people who have more than one hearth culture and find out how they deal with it. That might help the most.

Of course, your personal religion might be so eclectic that no single God, Goddess, or pantheon will ever be able to call you "theirs". You may belong to all the Gods and Goddesses, all the pantheons, and all the hearth cultures. If that's the case, then we wish you luck.

This is, of course, too much for most people to do in one sitting. You might just write down as many answers as you can now, and return to this later. Answering these questions, though, will be very helpful in trying to work through your Dedicant Oath, so bookmark the page!

Week 35: The Sixth High Holy Day: An Explanation

Related to Requirement: #2 – Meaning and Discussion of High Days
Required Reading:
- *Our Own Druidry*, p. 60 – 72 (Hearth Cultures & High Days)
- *ADF Constitution*, Article 4
- *The ADF Core Order of Ritual for High Days*,
  <http://www.adf.org/rituals/explanations/core-order.html>

Optional Reading:
- *Our Own Druidry*, p. 49 – 73 (The Very Basics of Ritual);
- *Appendix 1: Resources and Rituals for the Wheel of the Year* in this book;
- Step by Step through a Druid Worship Ceremony,
  <http://www.adf.org/rituals/explanations/stepbystep.html>;
- The "Liturgy and Rituals" section of the ADF page,
  <http://www.adf.org/rituals/>
- The Three Cranes Grove, ADF, outline of ritual (with example prayers),
  <http://www.threecranes.org/liturgy/>
- *The Crane Breviary and Guide Book* from the Order of the Crane:
  <https://www.adf.org/system/files/members/orders/crane/print/cbgb-preview.pdf>
- Rev. Skip Ellison's *The Solitary Druid*, appropriate high day in Chapters 6 & 7
- Nicholas Egelhoff's *Sunna's Journey: Norse Liturgy Through the Wheel of the Year*, appropriate High Day description

Welcome to your sixth High Holy Day as an ADF Dedicant. Next week's lesson will be a recap of the rite you do for this holiday.

If your culture does not celebrate a specific feast, remember that most cultures had a festival or feast that would have been similar in intent and form, but it may have been celebrated at a different time of year. Unfortunately, much of the work of discovering which festival might match up to which High Day must be left to the individual Dedicant. Your mentor, of course is available for some help, but we urge you to seek out one of the culture-specific email lists to ask questions on. Quite often, they will be of more help than your mentor can be.

The eight High Days are outlined on pages 60 – 72 of *Our Own Druidry*. If you are not of a Celtic hearth culture or you simply wish to expand your horizons and try a different culture because you are unsure what to do, locate a feast that seems appropriate, where it gives a short description of the feast. Take that description and work to find a compatible feast in your hearth culture for that particular High Day.

A lot of the High Holy Days are obviously agrarian-based. If the High Day feels "irrelevant," seek our relevance. Can you find the rhythms of nature in the city? Look hard for them, and I'll bet you can find something fresh and new in your climate that corresponds with this season.

Homework:

Now, in your Dedicant Notebook, reflect on this High Holy Day. Consider how it is celebrated in your hearth culture, or across hearth cultures. Are there any myths that are celebrated in connection with this feast? If so, what are they, and how do they fit in? What does this holiday or time of year mean to you? Do you look forward to it? Are there secular aspects of the holiday that mean a lot to you, or perhaps holdovers or memories of your childhood that you cherish? How do you know when this day arrives? Do you look at the calendar, or do you just *know* it has come? If you have children (or wish to have children), what key traditions do you wish to pass down to them? What, if anything, is spiritual or religious to you about this High Day or time of year, and how do you show that? Are there any traditions that your Grove has for this High Day? Finally, is there anything else about this holiday that you would like to add?

There, you've just written another essay on a High Holy Day, and you're moving along nicely through the Wheel of the Year.

If you have a local Grove that you attend, then you should already have a rite you can attend. If you are solitary (and even if you do have a Grove, I still recommend), though, you will need to write and perform your own ritual for this rite. Because only four High Days are required to be done as ADF rituals, you don't need to be too concerned with exactly how to do an ADF rite, but you should certainly have something written up, or else go to the ADF website and find a ritual that will fit your hearth culture and use that. We do not expect you to be a skilled liturgist this early in the journey. Make sure that you have a rite ready before you intend to do the ritual, though, because last minute ritual writing is never fun for anyone.

See Appendix 1 for more information on what the High Day is about, where we have provided a number of links to help you think about the High Days themselves (and included places to find some example rituals for you to work from!)

Also, continue visiting the spot that helps keep you connected to Nature. You might make notes in your Dedicant Notebook about what you see, or if there are animals that appear often or plants that strike you as intriguing or odd. Make sure that you also record any experiences of power or sudden flashes of insight that you might have.

Finally, are you still doing meditation? You're no longer required to, of course, but you are encouraged to continue the meditation and your journaling.

Week 36: Sixth High Day Recap

Related to Requirement: #8 – High Days Attended
Required Reading: None.

You've made it through your sixth ritual, which means there are only two more for you to go through during this turn of the wheel of the year! Congratulations! It's now time to add to your essays for the Dedicant Path documentation by writing a recap of the rite!

Homework:

First, we've provided a sort of ritual write-up template that will help you get all the commonly needed details down in Appendix 2. You cannot just turn in a number of those sheets and expect to pass this requirement, though: you need to be much more in-depth. So grab some paper and start thinking about the rite by asking some good questions.

Let's start out with an easy one: how did the rite go in terms of structure? What things went wrong during the ritual? What things went right? Who were the patrons of the rite, and who was the gatekeeper? Did you have problems with saying the words without stumbling, or did everything come out smoothly? Did you forget to bring a sacrifice? Were you alone, or with a group? If you were with a group, did you say anything or do anything? Now, for the not so easy part: how did the rite go in terms of function and feeling? Did you feel anything during the ritual? Did you experience doubt or confidence? Can you describe what happened? If you were with a group, what did the other people say about what happened? What omens were drawn (if any), and what did they tell you? Could you feel the presence of any deities, spirits, or powers? What else about the rite struck you, or do you want to share?

If you answer those questions, you've just finished another essay for the Dedicant Path documentation!

Also, make sure you're still visiting your natural space, and taking notes as you go. The notes will help greatly when you go to write your final essay on Nature Awareness.

Week 37: Home Shrine Revisited, Final Essay

Related to Requirement: #4 – Home Shrine; #10 – Personal Religion

Suggested Reading:

- *Oak Leaves* issue #14, "On the Solitary Path" by Judith Anderson Morris (Ladytoad) <http://www.adf.org/articles/solitary/ol-14.html>
- "Inserting Images into Text Documents" at <https://www.adf.org/members/training/submission-tips/images.html>

At this point, we're going to write the final essay regarding your Home Shrine. Keep in mind, though, that though this is the final essay, it is not the final example of your Shrine: it will continue to evolve as your spirituality evolves.

Homework:

Take pictures of your Home Shrine. Make careful note of anything that was added or subtracted from last time, and think about how it looks.

Now, let's look at the requirement for your essay:

"4. A brief description, with photos if possible, of the Dedicant's home shrine and plans for future improvements. (150 words min.)"

For this requirement, all you really need to do is provide three things, one of which is optional:

1. A brief description
2. Plans for improvement
3. Photos (optional)

I would highly, highly encourage you to send a photo with your work. Not only does it help make your description more complete, it also gives your reviewer a good idea of things you might forget to mention. There is, however, generally no need to send many photos; often, one will do just fine.

[**Note on photo submission:** Please try and re-size your photos[5] before sending them electronically or embedding them into a document to ensure that the files can be received. If you're not sure how to do this, please contact the ADF Preceptor prior to sending the photos to see if the size is okay.]

---

[5] If you don't know how to do this, please see "Inserting Images into Text Documents" at https://www.adf.org/members/training/submission-tips/images.html

When you describe what's on your altar, make sure that you mention everything you have on it, of course. Some things that you might forget though, are very valuable to your reviewer understanding your Shrine. What room is the altar in? Why did you pick each piece? Do the pieces have some sort of sentimental value? Why are the pieces arranged like they are? Do you decorate the altar differently for various seasons? How tall is it, and do you like the height? How often do you use the altar? Does it face a particular direction?

One of the biggest omissions in submissions is the plan for improvement. Altars are almost never done (though if you're positive yours is, feel free to say so!), and we can always think of things we would like to do, either when we have more space or more money (or both). Do you want to move it outside? Does that mean you'll need rain-proof statues? Are you searching for or thinking of commissioning deity representations? Is there an altar you've seen that you would like to duplicate? Would you like to add more altars around the house, or specific altars to specific deities?

Answer those questions, and you've finished another requirement!

Week 38: The Nine Virtues: Hospitality

Related to Requirement: #1 – Nine Virtues

Required Reading:

- *Our Own Druidry*, p. 13 ("Virtue, Piety and Study" & "Nine Pagan Virtues");
- *Our Own Druidry*, p. 81-86 ("Lore and Essays")

Optional Reading:

- A Virtuous Life Nine Virtues study guide by Rev. Michael J Dangler: <https://www.adf.org/system/files/members/training/dp/publications/dp-req-1-nine-virtues.pdf>;
- "Havamal": <http://www.pitt.edu/~dash/havamal.html>
- *Sacred Gifts: Reciprocity and the Gods* by Rev. Kirk Thomas

Welcome to the seventh of the Nine Virtues, hospitality! Hospitality is, of course, the first in the third triad I explained in week 13, the triad that corresponds to the producing class. You might consider going back to read through Week 13's lesson to get a background if you have forgotten some of it.

Something important to think about is the definition of the root word for both "guest" and "host", the Proto-Indo-European ***ghos-ti-***. Here is the definition from The American Heritage College Dictionary, the Proto-Indo-European appendix:

ghos-ti- Stranger, guest, host; properly "someone with whom one has reciprocal duties of hospitality." **1.** Basic for **ghos-ti-*. **a.** *(i)* GUEST, from Old Norse *gestr*, guest; *(ii)* GASTARBEITER, from Old High German *gast*, guest. Both *(i)* and *(ii)* from Germanic **gastiz*; **b.** HOST[2], HOSTILE, from Latin *hostis*, enemy (< "stranger"). **2.** Compound **ghos-pot-*, **ghos-po(d)-* "guest-master," one who symbolizes the relationship of reciprocal obligation (**pot-*, master; see **poti-**). HOSPICE, HOSPITABLE, HOSPITAL, HOSPITALITY, HOST[1], HOSTAGE, HOSTEL, HOSTLER, from Latin *hospes* (stem *hospit-*), host, guest, stranger. **3.** Suffixed zero-grade form **ghs-en-wo-*. XENIA, EXNO-, XENON; AXENIC, PROXENE, from Greek *xenos*, guest, host, stranger. [Pokorny *ghosti-s* 453.]

It seems like a lot of arcane wording, but if you can work your way through it, it might be helpful to you when you go to write your essay.

Basically, the word "Ghosti" has been adopted in ADF for the concept of the reciprocal guest-host relationship. This relationship is central to our ritual structure and to the ways we interact with others, both as Groves and as individuals.

If you have gotten this far in ADF and have not purchased a copy of Rev. Kirk Thomas' *Sacred Gifts: Reciprocity and the Gods*, I cannot recommend highly enough that you go out and get a copy. It delves deeply into the understanding of hospitality in many IE cultures, and will greatly benefit your work on this essay, and within ADF.

Homework:

The *Dedicant Handbook* defines hospitality as follows: "Acting as both a gracious host and an appreciative guest, involving benevolence, friendliness, humor, and the honoring of "a gift for a gift.""

Read through that statement until you think you understand it. In your Dedicant Notebook, answer the following questions: Does that definition cover hospitality in your eyes? Is it simply having people over, or is there more to it?

What does the definition mean by "gracious" and "appreciative"? Do these terms sit well with you? Are they too vague, or perhaps too specific?

If that definition doesn't quite sit right with you, head to your nearest dictionary and read the definitions in that it provides. Write it down (it is strongly recommended that you include a dictionary definition in your final write-up). Do any of those definitions make sense? Can they encompass all that hospitality is?

Now think of your own personal view of hospitality. Try to write it down in words. Feel free to steal phrases from the dictionary or the Handbook if you need to. Can you come up with a definition of hospitality that makes good sense to you?

Now, think about people you know whom you would call "hospitable". Examine why you think of them that way: is it something they know, something they do or the way they did it, or something they have said? Is it something beyond this? Can you find words to describe it?

Does hospitality go beyond simply having friends over to your house? Does it involve offering them the best you have and making them feel welcome? What does the DP Handbook mean when it talks about "being an appreciative guest"? Is it talking about doing something specific, or saying "thank you"?

What are the specific obligations you think a host has? What about the obligations that a guest has? Do both sides have obligations? How are these obligations related? Refer back to the *ghos-ti-* relationship outlined above. What is the connection there? How does the reciprocity work?

Think about myths and legends from different cultures. How was hospitality shown in the myths and legends? Was there a character in a myth that showed real hospitality? How was that hospitality displayed (in the Irish Cycles, Cu Chulann accepts a meal that will later lead to his death; how does this fit with your idea of hospitality)?

The Ghosti Relationship

The word ***ghos-ti*** is the Proto-Indo-European word which refers to the reciprocal relationships of hospitality. In fact, the English words "guest" and "host" both come from this root (the * at the beginning of the word just means that it's a word reconstructed by linguists and not attested in literature or archeology).

Our religion in ADF is based on this idea, that we can form relationships with the Powers by making offerings to Them, with the expectation that we may receive blessings and wisdom from Them in return.

—*Rev. Kirk Thomas*

Do you see yourself as a hospitable person? Hospitable in some ways but not others, perhaps? Not hospitable at all? Does one need to show hospitality consistently to understand the concept of hospitality, or to wonder about hospitality? Can anyone have hospitality?

Think of a time when you have exemplified this virtue. How did you feel? Did you know that this was a virtue at the time? Now think about a time when you failed to show this virtue. How did that make you feel? Did you feel as if you'd done something wrong or inadequate?

Finally, is hospitality a Virtue? Is it one that you agree should be on ADF's list? Why was it chosen? What is it about hospitality that either makes it a Virtue or keeps it from being one? If you have decided that it is not a Virtue, would you suggest another term, removing it altogether, or replacing it with something else entirely?

Now, go back through your answers to these questions and form a response of at least 125 words to "describe your understanding of the Virtue of hospitality."

And you have your seventh virtues essay out of the way!

Week 39: Nature Awareness (Final Essay)

Related to Requirement: #7 – Nature Awareness; #10 – Personal Religion
Required Reading: None

You've now been visiting your spot in nature for over thirty weeks, and you should have a very good idea of how you interact with that spot, and what goes on there. Now, it's time to think that through and turn out an essay!

Homework:

The requirement reads as follows:

"An account of the Dedicant's efforts to work with nature, honor the Earth, and understand the impacts and effects of the Dedicant's lifestyle choices on the environment and/or the local ecosystem and how she or he could make a difference to the environment on a local level. (500 word min)"

The requirement itself asks a lot of questions. Because you're probably going overboard in terms of sheer information at this point, this will probably work in your advantage.

Breaking it down, we have the following points:

1. Describe your efforts to work with nature
2. Describe how you honor the Earth
3. Give an understanding of how your lifestyle affects the environment/ecosystem
4. Describe how you can make a difference on a local level.

Now, you've got 500 words or so to do that. Here is where you might start:

First, talk about your connection to nature. How do you connect? Do you go to a specific place? Is that place mental or physical? Can you find yourself connected in the city? What makes up nature to you? Do you meditate in nature? Are you able to find a connection? If not, what have you tried to obtain one? Do you usually have a very strong connection to nature, but sometimes not manage to connect at all? What do you do then? Is nature something that you *always* feel connected to? Is this a result of where you live, or lifestyle choices you made?

Second, talk about how you honor the Earth. Here, you can talk about the Earth Mother as a Goddess, archetype, or mother. You can describe your concept of the sacred Earth, and discuss whether you find the Earth or Nature or the Universe to be something you worship or simply honor. Is honor something simple, like not littering, or is it more complicated, like organizing Earth Day events? When you think of "honoring" the Earth, what is it you think of?

Third, how do you live on the earth *right now*? Describe your lifestyle to some extent. If this different from how you lived on the earth when you started the DP, describe any changes you have already made. Do you see things you'd like to change? How much trash do you create, and do you recycle? Is this important to you? Where does your power come from, and do you have alternative energy choices? Are there wetlands near your house that have a sewage overflow? How do you take care of your landscaping and how do you water your plants/lawn? Are you doing things efficiently?

Finally, the fourth part is rather subjective: you need to consider what meant by "make a difference". What size difference are we talking about? What feels right to you? To make a difference, you could do something as simple as start recycling, or something as complex as joining a local environmental action group. So, first, you need to figure out what kind of difference is important to you, and then you need to figure out how to execute that. Note that it doesn't say, "Describe how you will make a difference", but now you "could" make a difference. There is no requirement for you to actually do it (though we would encourage you to do so). Make sure you're clear on what difference you would like to make, and how you would like to achieve that difference.

If you have all that down and have more than 500 words, you've just finished another requirement!

Next week, **your second book report is due**, so finish it up if you haven't already!

Week 40: Third Book Started: Hearth Culture

Related to Requirement: #3 – Book Reviews
Required Reading:

- *Our Own Druidry*, p. 17 – 18 ("Concerning the Reading of Books")
- *Our Own Druidry*, Appendix B, p. xiii ("Writing a Book Review")
- start on one book from the list of Hearth Culture titles at the ADF Website, <u>A Recommended Reading List</u>:
  <https://www.adf.org/training/resources/reading.html>

One of the reasons many people come to ADF is because they are looking for a religion or organization that is interested in both piety and study. Because this is a rare combination in the Neo-Pagan community, we are very proud to offer such things. We do expect our Dedicants to be well-versed in the basic scholarship behind ADF, the modern Neo-Pagan movement, and the historical roots of Neo-Paganism in general.

To this end, three book reviews are asked of all Dedicants, one in Indo-European studies (because ADF is an Indo-European based organization), one general Neo-Pagan movement book (because we are Neo-Pagan), and one book on one of the Indo-European hearth cultures (generally the hearth culture that the Dedicant will choose to work with).

We will work on the Hearth Culture title as your next book. The main idea is to help you understand more fully the intricacies and the specifics of the culture your Gods (or perhaps the Gods you're interested in) were worshipped in. If you have not chosen a hearth culture for your own practice yet, simply choose to read about a culture that interests you. The book you chose has absolutely no bearing on the hearth culture you choose.

As we do not expect you to finish the book you choose in one week, we will give you questions to think about now, and will remind you occasionally throughout the coming weeks to continue reading. The book review for this title will be due on Week 49.

By this point, you should have written up your review for your IE studies book and your Modern Paganism title. If you have not, here is a refresher for what you should cover in the book review (and please keep them in mind as you begin this final book):

Remember to start all book reviews with the bibliographical information. What is the book about? Is there a main thesis? Can you summarize the main points? Why was this book on the reading list? Do you think it should be there? Does it inform your own personal practice in any way? Does it give you new ideas, crazy thoughts, or open your mind? Could you recommend this book to others? Do you have trouble understanding it, or is it a breeze? Are there things that would make it better?

Making an outline or notes as you read will be invaluable to writing your book review later.

Keep these questions in mind as you read through the book, and let your mentor know what you're reading so he or she can help answer any questions you might have!

Week 41: The Seventh High Holy Day: An Explanation

Related to Requirement: #2 – Meaning and Discussion of High Days
Required Reading:

- *Our Own Druidry*, p. 60 – 72 (Hearth Cultures & High Days)
- *ADF Constitution*, Article 4
- *The ADF Core Order of Ritual for High Days*,
  <http://www.adf.org/rituals/explanations/core-order.html>

Optional Reading:

- *Our Own Druidry*, p. 49 – 73 (The Very Basics of Ritual);
- *Appendix 1: Resources and Rituals for the Wheel of the Year* in this book;
- Step by Step through a Druid Worship Ceremony,
  <http://www.adf.org/rituals/explanations/stepbystep.html>;
- The "Liturgy and Rituals" section of the ADF page,
  <http://www.adf.org/rituals/>
- The Three Cranes Grove, ADF, outline of ritual (with example prayers),
  <http://www.threecranes.org/liturgy/>
- *The Crane Breviary and Guide Book* from the Order of the Crane:
  <https://www.adf.org/system/files/members/orders/crane/print/cbgb-preview.pdf>
- Rev. Skip Ellison's *The Solitary Druid*, appropriate high day in Chapters 6 & 7
- Nicholas Egelhoff's *Sunna's Journey: Norse Liturgy Through the Wheel of the Year*, appropriate High Day description

Welcome to your seventh High Holy Day as an ADF Dedicant. Next week's lesson will be a recap of the rite you do for this holiday

If your culture does not celebrate a specific feast, remember that most cultures had a festival or feast that would have been similar in intent and form, but it may have been celebrated at a different time of year. Unfortunately, much of the work of discovering which festival might match up to which High Day must be left to the individual Dedicant. Your mentor, of course is available for some help, but we urge you to seek out one of the culture-specific email lists to ask questions on. Quite often, they will be of more help than your mentor can be.

The eight High Days are outlined on pages 60 – 72 of *Our Own Druidry*. If you are not of a Celtic hearth culture or you simply wish to expand your horizons and try a different culture because you are unsure what to do, locate a ritual that seems appropriate, where it gives a short description of the feast. Take that description and work to find a compatible feast in your hearth culture for that particular High Day.

A lot of the High Holy Days are obviously agrarian-based. If the High Day feels "irrelevant," seek our relevance. Can you find the rhythms of nature in the city? Look hard for them, and I'll bet you can find something fresh and new in your climate that corresponds with this season.

Homework:

Now, in your Dedicant Notebook, reflect on this High Holy Day. Consider how it is celebrated in your hearth culture, or across hearth cultures. Are there any myths that are celebrated in connection with this feast? If so, what are they, and how do they fit in? What does this holiday or time of year mean to you? Do you look forward to it? Are there secular aspects of the holiday that mean a lot to you, or perhaps holdovers or memories of your childhood that you cherish? How do you know when this day arrives? Do you look at the calendar, or do you just *know* it has come? If you have children (or wish to have children), what key traditions do you wish to pass down to them? What, if anything, is spiritual or religious to you about this High Day or time of year, and how do you show that? Are there any traditions that your Grove has for this High Day? Finally, is there anything else about this holiday that you would like to add?

There, you've just written another essay on a High Holy Day, and there is only one more to go!

If you have a local Grove that you attend, then you should already have a rite you can attend. If you are solitary (and even if you do have a Grove, I still recommend), though, you will need to write and perform your own ritual for this rite. Because only four High Days are required to be done as ADF rituals, you don't need to be too concerned with exactly how to do an ADF rite, but you should certainly have something written up, or else go to the ADF website and find a ritual that will fit your hearth culture and use that. We do not expect you to be a skilled liturgist this early in the journey. Make sure that you have a rite ready before you intend to do the ritual, though, because last minute ritual writing is never fun for anyone.

See Appendix 1 for more information on what the High Day is about, where we have provided a number of links to help you think about the High Days themselves (and included places to find some example rituals for you to work from!)

Week 42: Seventh High Day Recap

Related to Requirement: #8 – High Days Attended
Required Reading: None.

You've made it through your seventh ritual, which means there is only one more for you to go through during this turn of the wheel of the year! Congratulations! It's now time to add to your essays for the Dedicant Path documentation by writing a recap of the rite!

Homework:

First, we've provided a sort of ritual write-up template that will help you get all the commonly needed details down in Appendix 2. You cannot just turn in a number of those sheets and expect to pass this requirement, though: you need to be much more in-depth. So grab some paper and start thinking about the rite by asking some good questions.

Let's start out with an easy one: how did the rite go in terms of structure? What things went wrong during the ritual? What things went right? Who were the patrons of the rite, and who was the gatekeeper? Did you have problems with saying the words without stumbling, or did everything come out smoothly? Did you forget to bring a sacrifice? Were you alone, or with a group? If you were with a group, did you say anything or do anything? Now, for the not so easy part: how did the rite go in terms of function and feeling? Did you feel anything during the ritual? Did you experience doubt or confidence? Can you describe what happened? If you were with a group, what did the other people say about what happened? What omens were drawn (if any), and what did they tell you? Could you feel the presence of any deities, spirits, or powers? What else about the rite struck you, or do you want to share?

If you answer those questions, you've just finished another essay for the Dedicant Path documentation!

Week 43: The Three Kindred: Deities

Related to Requirement: #7 – Nature Awareness; #9 – Relationships to Kindred; #10 – Personal Religion

Required reading:

- *Our Own Druidry*, p. 25 ("The Shining Ones");
- *Our Own Druidry*, p. 41 – 42 ("The Shining Ones")

Optional Reading:

- *The Solitary Druid* by Rev. Skip Ellison, p. 17 – 19 ("The Mighty Kindred")
- *Sacred Fire, Holy Well* by Ian Corrigan, p. 16 ("The Shining Ones"), p. 25 – 26 ("Concerning the Gods"), p. 35 – 48 ("The Gods of Pagan Eire" & "A Celtic Pantheon")

The Shining Ones. The Gods and Goddesses of Elder Days. First Children of the Mother. The Gods of This Place. The Great Ones. The Elder Ones. Eldest and Wisest.

For the Deities, we have many titles. They form a vital part of our worship, and our liturgy treats them as objective entities who are worthy of our worship. We form bonds between ourselves and the gods that involve a system of reciprocity and blessings.

Often, we limit the deities we worship to those from our hearth culture. Some limit them even further to their Patrons only. There are often deities that we forget about, though.

There are deities of place, beings who were here before us and were worshipped by the native peoples. There are deities of our tribe (or, more likely in our case, our Grove) who we worship because they are part of our family. Finally, there are the gods and goddesses of our personal lives, those who guide us and protect us.

There are many theories held by ADF members about the nature of the gods. As mentioned above, our liturgies refer to the gods as real things, things that exist outside our heads, taking a stance often referred to as "hard polytheism." In actual practice, some members agree with this, others do not. ADF does not require you to accept deity as "real" beyond your mind. That's just how we deal with them ritually.

Homework:

Think about how you interact with the deities. What do you call it when you do ritual? Is it "worship" to the Gods, "honor" to the Gods, or "love" to the Gods? Or is it something else entirely? Are these terms even different to you?

When you think of your place in the cosmos, relative to where the Gods are, what is the relationship? Are the Gods above you, around you, inside you? Do they take an active part in your life? Can you map out where they are graphically? Do they reside in a physical place (like the Mt. Olympus of the Greeks)?

Do you think on the deities when you are going through your daily life? Do you worship them often with no request for a return blessing, or are you more often asking for something than providing selfless worship (it's okay if you are)?

If you could tell someone one thing about the nature of the Gods, what would it be? Try and explain it in a paragraph, then in a sentence, and then in a single word. Does it work?

Write all this in your Dedicant Notebook. We'll refer back to it in Week 46, when we look at writing our essay about the Three Kindred.

Week 44: The Nine Virtues: Moderation

Related to Requirement: #1 – Nine Virtues

Required Reading:

- *Our Own Druidry*, p. 13 ("Virtue, Piety and Study" & "Nine Pagan Virtues");
- *Our Own Druidry*, p. 81-86 ("Lore and Essays")

Optional Reading:

- A Virtuous Life Nine Virtues study guide by Rev. Michael J Dangler: <https://www.adf.org/system/files/members/training/dp/publications/dp-req-1-nine-virtues.pdf>;
- *Real Magick* by Isaac Bonewits (1989 edition, ISBN: 0877286884), p. 13 (Two Minute Sermon on Drugs in Magic);
- *Druid's Progress* issue #8, "Pagans in Recovery" by Isaac Bonewits <http://www.adf.org/articles/philosophy/pagans-in-recovery.html>

Welcome to the eighth of the Nine Virtues, moderation! Moderation is, of course, the second in the third triad I explained in week 13, the triad that corresponds to the producing class. You might consider going back to read through Week 13's lesson to get a background if you have forgotten some of it.

Homework:

The Dedicant Handbook defines moderation as follows: "Cultivating one's appetites so that one is neither a slave to them nor driven to ill health (mental or physical), through excess or deficiency."

Read through that statement until you think you understand it. In your Dedicant Notebook, answer the following questions: Does that definition cover moderation in your eyes? Is it simply watching what you eat, or is there more to it?

What does the definition mean by "cultivating one's appetites" and "excess or deficiency"? Do these terms sit well with you? Are they too vague, or perhaps too specific?

If that definition doesn't quite sit right with you, head to your nearest dictionary and read the definitions in that it provides. Write it down (it is strongly recommended that you include a dictionary definition in your final write-up). Do any of those definitions make sense? Can they encompass all that moderation is?

Now think of your own personal view of moderation. Try to write it down in words. Feel free to steal phrases from the dictionary or the Handbook if you need to. Can you come up with a definition of moderation that makes good sense to you?

Now, think about people you know whom you would call "moderate". Examine why you think of them that way: is it something they know, something they do or the way they did it, or something they have said? Is it something beyond this? Can you find words to describe it?

Does moderation go beyond simply having friends over to your house? Does it involve offering them the best you have and making them feel welcome? What does the DP Handbook mean when it talks about "cultivating one's appetite"? Is it talking about doing something specific, or a general idea of training yourself?

Think about myths and legends from different cultures. How was moderation shown in the myths and legends? Was there a character in a myth that showed real moderation? How was that moderation displayed (in the Rome, Cincinnatus gives up the kingship of Rome and goes back to his plow; how does this fit with your idea of moderation)?

Do you see yourself as a moderate person? Moderate in some ways but not others, perhaps? Not moderate at all? Does one need to show moderation consistently to understand the concept of moderation, or to wonder about moderation? Can anyone have moderation?

Moderation is most often defined in terms of not drinking too much, or perhaps not eating too much. Are there other arenas where this is more important? Why is there such an emphasis on alcohol and foods? Does this emphasis cause us not to think about other kinds of moderation?

Think of a time when you have exemplified this virtue. How did you feel? Did you know that this was a virtue at the time? Now think about a time when you failed to show this virtue. How did that make you feel? Did you feel as if you'd done something wrong or inadequate?

Finally, is moderation a Virtue? Is it one that you agree should be on ADF's list? Why was it chosen? What is it about moderation that either makes it a Virtue or keeps it from being one? If you have decided that it is not a Virtue, would you suggest another term, removing it altogether, or replacing it with something else entirely?

Now, go back through your answers to these questions and form a response of at least 125 words to "describe your understanding of the Virtue of moderation."

And you have your eighth of nine Virtues essay out of the way!

Week 45: The Nine Virtues: Fertility

Related to Requirement: #1 – Nine Virtues
Required Reading:

- *Our Own Druidry*, p. 13 ("Virtue, Piety and Study" & "Nine Pagan Virtues");
- *Our Own Druidry*, p. 81-86 ("Lore and Essays")

Optional Reading:

- A Virtuous Life Nine Virtues study guide by Rev. Michael J Dangler: <https://www.adf.org/system/files/members/training/dp/publications/dp-req-1-nine-virtues.pdf>;
- The Man Who Planted Trees by Jean Giono <http://home.infomaniak.ch/arboretum/Man_Tree.htm>

Welcome to the ninth of the Nine Virtues, fertility! Fertility is, of course, the third in the third triad I explained in week 13, the triad that corresponds to the producing class. You might consider going back to read through Week 13's lesson to get a background if you have forgotten some of it.

Homework:

The Dedicant Handbook defines fertility as follows: "Bounty of mind, body and spirit, involving creativity, production of objects, food, works of art, etc., an appreciation of the physical, sensual, nurturing"

Read through that statement until you think you understand it. In your Dedicant Notebook, answer the following questions: Does that definition cover fertility in your eyes? Is it simply having people over, or is there more to it?

What does the definition mean by "creativity" and "appreciation of the physical"? Do these terms sit well with you? Are they too vague, or perhaps too specific?

If that definition doesn't quite sit right with you, head to your nearest dictionary and read the definitions in that it provides. Write it down (it is strongly recommended that you include a dictionary definition in your final write-up). Do any of those definitions make sense? Can they encompass all that fertility is?

Now think of your own personal view of fertility. Try to write it down in words. Feel free to steal phrases from the dictionary or the Handbook if you need to. Can you come up with a definition of fertility that makes good sense to you?

Now, think about people you know whom you would call "fertile". Examine why you think of them that way: is it something they know, something they do or the way they did it, or something they have said? Is it something beyond this? Can you find words to describe it?

Does fertility go beyond simply having creativity and/or having children? Does it involve physical creation and bringing ideas to fruition? What does the DP Handbook mean when it talks about "an appreciation of the physical, sensual, nurturing"? Is it talking about doing something specific, and how does this fit in with the idea of creativity?

Think about myths and legends from different cultures. How was fertility shown in the myths and legends? Was there a character in a myth that showed real fertility? How was that fertility displayed (in the Greek myth, Oranus rains upon Gaia, creating life; how does this fit with your idea of fertility)?

Do you see yourself as a fertile person? Fertile in some ways but not others, perhaps? Not fertile at all? Does one need to show fertility consistently to understand the concept of fertility, or to wonder about fertility? Can anyone have fertility?

Think of a time when you have exemplified this virtue. How did you feel? Did you know that this was a virtue at the time? Now think about a time when you failed to show this virtue. How did that make you feel? Did you feel as if you'd done something wrong or inadequate?

Finally, is fertility a Virtue? Is it one that you agree should be on ADF's list? Why was it chosen? What is it about fertility that either makes it a Virtue or keeps it from being one? If you have decided that it is not a Virtue, would you suggest another term, removing it altogether, or replacing it with something else entirely? Many ADF members have issues with this particular Virtue. Why do you think that is?

Now, go back through your answers to these questions and form a response of at least 125 words to "describe your understanding of the Virtue of fertility."

And you have your final virtues essay finished! Congratulations!

Week 46: The Three Kindred: Final Essays

Related to Requirement: #7 – Nature Awareness; #9 – Relationships to Kindred; #10 – Personal Religion

Required Reading:
- *Our Own Druidry*, p. 26 – 28 (Nine Holy Things)
- *Our Own Druidry*, p. 43 – 45 (The Spirits in the Land)

Over the past 48 weeks, you have spent time in intimate contact with the Nature Spirits, experienced festivals devoted to the Ancestors, and done right worship to the Goddesses and Gods. By now, you should have a good understanding of these three Kindred. This week, we will work on articulating that in your final essay about these three groups.

Make sure you have your notes from weeks 12, 32, and 43 handy.

Homework:

The requirement we will be answering today is this:

"9. ONE essay describing the Dedicants understanding of and relationship to EACH of the Three Kindred: the Spirits of Nature, the Ancestors and the Gods. (300 words min. for each Kindred and 1000 words total)"

Examining this requirement, we have a simple breakdown of one major essay in three parts. This is listed as one essay because these three Kindred are interwoven and tied together; they are not three separate groups that act independently of each other.

In this essay, you will be expected to write about each of the Three Kindred:

- The Spirits of Nature
- The Ancestors
- The Gods

For each of the Three Kindred, you will be expected to show not only an "understanding" of who/what they are, but also talk about your "personal relationship" with these Kindred. This means that it is not enough to simply speak in general terms about them, but you will need to speak personally about what they mean to you.

Some things that can help you when you consider each of these Three Kindred as you write your essay are the following:

For each of the Three Kindred, think about the following questions (not all may apply, but taking a moment to think about them might help you articulate something):

- Which of the Three Realms is this Kindred associated with?
- Which of the Three Worlds is this Kindred associated with?
- Which of the ritual Gates (Fire, Well, Tree) is this Kindred associated with?

- Which power(s) in the Two Powers meditation is this Kindred associated with?
- What places are sacred to this Kindred?
- If you are not in a place that is sacred to this Kindred, how do you contact them from there?
- Where can you contact this Kindred?
- Are there myths or legends about this Kindred that give you insight into its nature?
- The Kindred often have many titles. What do these titles reflect?
- What sort of offerings do you give to this Kindred?
- What do you call on this Kindred for?
- What is the nature of this Kindred's relationship to humans?
- What is the nature of this Kindred's relationship to other the other Kindred?

Think of times that you personally have interacted with the members of this Kindred. What sort of feelings did you get? How did you interact with them? Did your interaction with them change how you saw them? How are you related to this Kindred? Is there a time when this Kindred has really helped you out? Is there a time when you felt a real connection to them?

How do the myths portray this Kindred? What do the cultures you have studied have to say about them? Does what they say resound in you?

Make sure you address each of the Three Kindred in turn, and that you describe both your understanding and your experience of the Kindred in question. Some general talk about the Kindred will also benefit you (such as similarities between them, or wide differences).

Now, the hard part: boiling all of this down into one essay. You need to provide at least 100 words about the Three Kindred in general, including their relationship to each other. Beyond that, take all those questions that we applied to the Kindred above, and boil them down to 300 word responses about each. *Remember to talk about your personal relationship with them!*

Once you've done that, you'll have your essay done on the Three Kindred!

A Prayer to the Three Kindreds

My Spirit is the Spirit of my Ancestors:
Their blood is my blood, their heart is my heart.

My eyes see the wonder of the world they left to me,
And I shall leave it to my children better than I found it.
Hail the Ancestors!

My Spirit is the Spirit of the Nature-Kin:
Their joy is my joy, their song my song.

My steps go lightly in deference to them,
That I may walk among them in honor.
Hail the Nature Spirits!

My Spirit is the Spirit of the Gods and Goddesses
Their wisdom is my wisdom, their prayer my prayer

My life is lived in honor of them,
Maintaining the order of the worlds through sacrifice.
Hail the Shining Ones!

Art by Ian Corrigan, Prayer by Rev. Michael J Dangler | www.threecranes.org

Week 47: Wrapping Up: Personal Religion (Final Essay) and Book Reports

Related to Requirement: #10 – Personal Religion
Required Reading:

- *Our Own Druidry*, p. 17 ("The Hearth Oath")
- *Our Own Druidry*, p. 117 – 122 ("Personalizing Your Paganism")
- *Our Own Druidry*, p. xv – xvi ("Appendix 1: Adapting the DP to Specific Ethnic Paths")

Optional reading:

- *Sacred Fire, Holy Well* by Ian Corrigan, p. 264 – 267 ("The Waiting Shrine") & p. 277 – 279 ("Working With the Patron")
- *Sacred Gifts* by Kirk Thomas, p. 182 – 201 ("Two Simple Rituals of Connection")

This week, we'll discuss your personal spirituality in preparation to writing and taking your Dedicant Oath.

We talked about this last in Week 35, where we pointed out that personal religion is just that: personal. No one can (or will) tell you how to worship. We may make suggestions, based primarily on what works for a lot of us, and we'll tell you about the way ADF does ritual, but we can't tell you how to worship on your own.

That said, let's look at ways to make you religion work best for you, and help you to answer the exit standard for the Dedicant Path documentation.

Also, if your book reports aren't done yet, now is the time to do them.

Homework:

First, finish any book reports you may have left over. There are only five weeks of DP work after this one, and you don't want to be rushing to finish them while trying to finish this work. If you need help writing them, see the required reading for this section and weeks 6, 26, and 42.

The requirement for the Personal Religion bit reads as follows:

"10. A brief account of the efforts of the Dedicant to develop and explore a personal (or Grove-centered) spiritual practice, drawn from a specific culture or combination of cultures." (600 words min.)

This requirement basically asks you to discuss your journey of personal exploration within Druidry. Isn't that nicely concise?

It's not as broad as it first appears, so let's make it more manageable.

First, the requirement talks about both personal and "Grove-centered" spiritual practice. These are not necessarily opposed things. Some people do not have access to a Grove (or choose to practice alone), and will thus be only able to focus on a personal practice. Some are fortunate enough to have a Grove that focuses on their hearth culture, which allows them to work exclusively with their Grove, and thus their needs do not include an extremely personal spirituality. Others will find that their Grove does not always work with their hearth culture, and so they require their own personal spirituality to compliment their Grove work.

Most Groves work with a "Pantheon of Agreement" that all members follow while in ritual. Each person may not worship those deities and Powers in their own personal religions, but they might work with them in order to obtain that community aspect of religion.

Start by thinking where you fall in this. Is your spirituality personal, or Grove-centered? Is it both? If it is centered on a Grove, is the Grove mostly or usually working in your hearth culture or in a set of cultures you are interested in? If not, how do you deal with this? Do you see Grove worship as a Pantheon of agreement?

Look back at the first week's lessons. Survey the questions there: how many answers do you still agree with? What do you think about your ideas and motivations? Would you change them? Try re-answering those questions from your current perspective.

Review your First Oath. Have you been true to it? Has it helped you through when you have had doubts? Does it seem outdated at this point? Write a reaction to it.

Back in week 8, you began creating your home shrine. How does this figure into your religious practice? Does it fit into your daily life? Do you use it for meditation? Do you still meditate? You have also written essays on the Nine Virtues. Do you use these in daily life? What lessons that you have learned do you continue to utilize in your personal religion? How has the DP helped?

Do you utilize ADF's core symbolism of Three Realms, Three Kindred, Three Worlds, Three Gates, etc.? Why or why not? If you use something else, what is it you use, and why do you use it?

If you have chosen a hearth culture, what is it? How did you choose it? What drew you to it? Was it a long process, or did you know it when you came in? Do you worship all the deities in that pantheon, and if not, which ones do you worship? How do you connect to that hearth culture?

How do your hearth cultures' values and religious worldview affect your own? Have you changed your personal spirituality to fit the ideals of a hearth culture (or two)?

Are there other aspects of your spiritual life you'd like to talk about? If you have another tradition (such as Wiccan or Discordian or Goddess Worship), how does that fit in with ADF?

Finally, ask yourself seriously if ADF and Neo-Pagan Druidism are right for you.

From those notes, write an essay that charts your spiritual growth from the time you began the work of an ADF Dedicant until now. Be sure to mention your growth, how your Grove (or lack of a Grove) has played into this, and what hearth cultures you have either settled on or are interested in.

And you're now one requirement away from finishing the Dedicant Path documentation!

Week 48: The Dedicant Oath

Related to Requirement: #11 – Dedicant Oath and Rite
Required Reading:

- *Our Own Druidry*, p. 129 – 130 (The Dedicant's Oath)

Optional Reading:

- Rev. Michael J Dangler's Dedicant Oath, <http://www.chronarchy.com/mjournal/oath/>;
- Raven Mann's Dedicant Oath, <http://www.adf.org/members/training/dp/examples/raven-mann/oath-rite.html>
- "Sealing an Oath: Adding a Dash of (Hearth) Culture," by Rev. Michael J Dangler <http://www.adf.org/members/training/dp/articles/sealing-an-oath.html>
- "Exploring Oaths," by Rev. James "Seamus" Dillard. *Oak Leaves* #53, p. 24-28 <https://www.adf.org/system/files/members/publications/oak-leaves/OL-53-Summer-2011.pdf>

We have left the Dedicant Oath until last because it is the crowning achievement of any Dedicant's work. In order to write this Oath, the Dedicant should have all the tools at their disposal that are possible: a complete understanding of ADF ritual (gained through working through the Wheel of the Year); a strong affinity for nature; a strong set of values; and understanding of their hearth culture (if chosen); an excellent scholarly background to build upon; and a relationship with the Three Kindred.

At this point, nearly a year into your work with ADF, you are not flying blind. You have completed all the other requirements, and you have a significant body of work behind you.

Most importantly, you know if you are on the right path.

Part of why last week's requirement asked you to seriously examine if Neo-Pagan Druidry is the right path for you is because if they is not, you should not take the Dedicant Oath.

This is fine. We do not expect the ADF Dedicant Path to be for everyone. If you have come this far, decided that ADF or Druidry is not right for you, and suddenly feel like you've been cheated by the Oath, then you're thinking about the Dedicant Path wrong. The DP is not a set of goals to complete, but a journey that we take. You've seen all the wonderful things it has to offer, and the journey isn't over, but has rather just begun. You may not finish the DP, but you have come to an understanding on the same level as one who has. There is nothing to be ashamed of in stopping here.

We do not expect you to swear allegiance to ADF, to the Archdruid, to a Grove, or anything like that. The Dedicant Oath is not to any single body, person, or thing. It is a dedication to the path of Neo-Pagan Druidry as your primary path. As has been stated before, this is not an exclusionary oath: if you have another path that is equally important to you, you should make sure that the wording of your oath is not one that prevents you from following that path.

It may sound confusing to say that Druidry is your "primary path", and yet it is still "non-exclusionary." "Neo-Pagan Druidry" is a very loosely defined path, and can include many things (including working in other organizations). Keep in mind, also, that ADF embraces a wide variety of Indo-European cultures as part of "Neo-Pagan Druidry."

Oaths that include dedication to concepts like the elder ways; the Three Kindreds; or the religion, magic, and gods and goddesses of one's forbears (or heart-kin) are in line with Neo-Pagan Druidry. Some fuzzier areas might include concepts like commitment to the Neopagan community, oaths to "Mother Earth" & "Father Sky," or general concepts of Pagan religion or spirituality. At the other end of the spectrum, it's possible for a Dedicant's Oath to be too specific. For example, a rite in which the student's sole purpose is to dedicate himself to one or more specific gods or goddesses—without further qualification—would not be appropriate as a Dedicant's Oath. (Which is not to say that sort of oath couldn't be *part* of a Dedicant's Oath). Nor would it be appropriate for a Dedicant to dedicate herself to ADF, the organization; it's the *path* that really matters, not the vehicle. Again, this is not to say that one couldn't include such a dedication as part of her oath—just that by itself, it would be inappropriate.

In the end, it's up to you exactly how you word the Oath. Don't spend your time thinking about how to work around it, though. Think about what you want to Oath, not what you don't want to Oath.

You will be required to provide the text of your Dedicant Oath, and that is what we will work on this week.

Homework:

Begin by looking at the sample Dedicant Oath listed on page 133 of *Our Own Druidry*. It is possible that the Oath text on that page will be exactly what you're looking for. More likely than not, though, it will be a source for good ideas and a starting point for your own.

If you have a hearth culture, you might look up traditions in that culture for Oathing. If there is a deity who presides over oaths (such as Thor) or a tool that is often used for oaths (like a ring or a hammer), you might incorporate that into your rite. A quick search of the internet will doubtless turn up a great number of hits (and, of course, take those with a grain of salt).

You might mention these tools and deities in the Oath itself. "By Thor's mighty hammer which I now hold, I Oath…" or "I call on Oath, Granddaughter of Night, to hear my words…" can help reinforce the words in your mind and impress them onto your soul.

Many people end their Oath by describing what will happen if they break their oath. Celtic-focused persons may say, "May the sea swallow me, the earth open below me, and the sky fall upon me if I break my oath!" Again, these statements help reinforce the Oath. The article "*Sealing an Oath: Adding a Dash of (Hearth) Culture*" will be helpful here.

You may also wish to bless a symbol of your dedication (a stone, necklace or ring perhaps), mention the item in your Oath, and call on the Powers witnessing your Oath to bless it and remind you of your Oath.

In the end, you will need to say what resonates with you. Make sure you can pronounce all names and the languages you use (this is not the time to try out Gaelic for the first time). It is good to address and sacrifice to each of the Three Kindreds, the Earth Mother, and any Patrons. Make the Oath feel right to you, because that is what is most important. Make sure it is specific and that it says exactly what you want it to say. Next week, we will prepare the rite around it.

Week 49: Final High Day and Dedicant Oath Rite

Related to Requirement: #2 – Meaning and Discussion of High Days; #9 – Relationships to Kindred; #10 – Personal Religion; #11 – Dedicant Oath and Rite
Required reading: None.

Ideally, your Dedicant Oath Rite will be public. You may or may not write and perform the entire rite yourself. Often, Groves will provide a section of the rite where the Oath can be given, and the Dedicant's only duty will be to pronounce her Oath. Sometimes, Groves who have several people going through the DP at once might have all their Dedicants speak their Oaths at the same rite and give them the responsibility of performing and administering every part of the rite. Solitary members might request to make their Oath at an ADF festival, reaffirming their connection to the rest of the organization (check with the Grove hosting to see if this is possible). Other Solitaries will do the rite as they have worked through the entire program: alone.

Each of these approaches is fine. While we encourage public performance, that is not always possible or even desirable, and as such we do not require it. It is up to the Dedicant to find (or create) the venue that is proper to them.

The Dedicant Oath Rite should be an ADF-style rite. Remember that this means that you should employ a triple center, and Indo-European focus, and other things common to ADF rites. Although it should go without saying, please also note that because this is an ADF rite, you should not use blood in the rite, *especially* if the rite is done publicly.

Page 124 of *Our Own Druidry* begins a ritual outline for a Dedicant Oath Rite. It is written for a solitary member, and you can lift the rite entirely if you wish. If you are working with a Grove, you might ask the Senior Druid to help you with figuring out what to do at the rite.

A few things need to be said. As with all rites, record your omens. It is vitally important here, and you should read the omens (or have the Grove Seer interpret them for you) as they refer to your personal path. Take the omen however you are comfortable (Runes, Tarot, or Ogham, or simply by flipping coins). Write down any insights you may have at the time, and review the omens again after the rite and write down any further interpretations you may have.

Record and have ready all sacrifices you will (or might) need for the ritual. Have some extra on hand just in case. Think carefully about appropriate offerings.

Homework:

Perform your rite.

You will be required to make a self-evaluation of the rite, including how you performed. Write down anything you can think of that was important. Then write down anything that seemed unimportant. Write down what went right and what went wrong. Get as complete a record as possible. We'll sort through it next week, when you finish your write-up.

By now, you should be comfortable with the order of ritual and you should know how to put one together. Make sure that you detail what this High Day is all about so that you can finish your requirement for describing the High Days. You will also need to finish your third book review.

Congratulations!

Week 50: Final High Day and Dedicant Oath Rite Recap

Related to Requirement: #8 – High Days Attended; #9 – Relationships to Kindred; #10 – Personal Religion; #11 – Dedicant Oath and Rite

Suggested Reading:

- "My Dedicant Oath" by Monika Butke,
  <http://www.adf.org/members/training/dp/articles/dedicant-oath-monika.html>

You've made it through your final ritual before becoming an ADF Dedicant, which means you have walked this Path during a single turn of the Wheel! Congratulations! It's now time to finish your essays for the Dedicant Path documentation by writing a recap of the rite!

Homework:

First, we've provided a sort of ritual write-up template that will help you get all the commonly needed details down in Appendix 2. You cannot just turn in a number of those sheets and expect to pass this requirement, though: you need to be much more in-depth. So grab some paper and start thinking about the rite by asking some good questions.

Let's start out with an easy one: how did the rite go in terms of structure? What things went wrong during the ritual? What things went right? Who were the patrons of the rite, and who was the gatekeeper? Did you have problems with saying the words without stumbling, or did everything come out smoothly? Did you forget to bring a sacrifice? Were you alone, or with a group? If you were with a group, did you say anything or do anything? Now, for the not so easy part: how did the rite go in terms of function and feeling? Did you feel anything during the ritual? Did you experience doubt or confidence? Can you describe what happened? If you were with a group, what did the other people say about what happened? What omens were drawn (if any), and what did they tell you? Could you feel the presence of any deities, spirits, or powers? What else about the rite struck you, or do you want to share? Make sure to include your Dedicant Oath text, too! Finally, where do you think you will go next in ADF?

If you answer those questions, you've just finished your final essay for the Dedicant Path documentation!

Week 51: Creating a Plan for Living Your Druidism

Recommended Reading:

- Rev. Kirk Thomas, "The DP – Milestone on a Wondrous Journey"
  <http://www.adf.org/members/training/dp/articles/dp-milestone.html>

We began the first week by discussing the journey that is the Dedicant Path, but the journey of an ADF Dedicant doesn't end with the Dedicant Oath. The Dedicant Oath, really, is the first step along the path of our living tradition of Neo-Pagan Druidry.

The ADF Dedicant Path documentation does not require that you continue with the exercises, meditations, and practices you've experienced over the past year. Your level of personal practice is up to you, and your practice is between you and your deities, not between you and ADF.

Start by going back to your original set of questions from Week 1. There, we asked a lot of questions about what you expected. Look over the answers, and get a feel for what they implied back then and what they mean to you now. Now, we're going to look at what you found, and what you expect now that you have finished your Dedicant studies.

1. Looking at all the things you've done, what was the hardest requirement to you? Was it one you expected? Do you feel that you fully understand the requirement, or is there room for improvement?
2. What was the easiest requirement for you? Do you feel that you learned something from it? Describe the value of the requirement in a way that has meaning to you.
3. Which requirement surprised you the most?
4. What things did you learn that you would most like to continue with?
5. Now that you have given your Dedicant Oath before your gods and your community, how do you see yourself living that Oath daily? What sort of things will you do to fulfill the Oath you took?
6. Have you considered starting a Grove (or helping to lead your current one)? Is there a leadership position in a Guild or a SIG that you're interested in? Would you like to run for an office in ADF?
7. Where do you see the skills you learned as a Dedicant being the most useful? Will they primarily be useful to you, your community, to ADF, or to other Dedicants?
8. What are the next goals you wish to set for yourself, either personally, spiritually, or within ADF?

The Dedicant Path documentation can be a huge personal accomplishment, but we challenge you to spend this weekend thinking about what this accomplishment means to you in three ways: how it impacts you personally, how it impacts your community, and how it impacts your deities. Spend some time meditating, or visiting your spot in nature, or simply contemplating these things. There is no further homework this week than just considering those connections.

Week 52: Final Recap, Submission, and The Road Ahead

Recommended Reading:

- *Dedicant Path FAQ,* <http://www.adf.org/members/training/dp/faq.html>

When you're ready to submit, get a mailing envelope large enough for your entire submission, and begin printing off your work.

Take a look at this checklist and ensure that you have all the following items in your submission packet (the list is divided by requirement):

- ❏ Essays for each of the Nine Virtues:
    - o Wisdom
    - o Piety
    - o Vision
    - o Courage
    - o Integrity
    - o Perseverance
    - o Hospitality
    - o Moderation
    - o Fertility
- ❏ Essays for each of the 8 High Days
    - o Samhain
    - o Winter Solstice
    - o Imbolc
    - o Spring Equinox
    - o Beltaine
    - o Summer Solstice
    - o Lughnassadh
    - o Autumnal Equinox
- ❏ Three book reviews
    - o IE Studies Title
    - o Ethnic Studies Title
    - o Modern Paganism Title
- ❏ Home Shrine
    - o Pictures (optional)
- ❏ Essay about the Two Powers
- ❏ Essay *or* journal for mental discipline
- ❏ Nature awareness essay
- ❏ Account of all High Days *attended or performed* in a 12 month period
- ❏ *One* essay covering each of the three Kindreds:
    - o Nature Spirits
    - o Ancestors

- o Deities
- ❑ Essay on personal religion
- ❑ Dedicant oath
  - o Text of the rite
  - o Self-evaluation of the rite

Once you ensure that you have all your items for submission, take all of your information (and you have ensured that each essay is complete and meets all the criteria), **back it up**, and ship it to the ADF Office.

Please submit an electronic copy of your work through the Study Program Tracker at https://www.adf.org/members/training/submissions/index.php. Please send only your completed Dedicant Path documentation. DP's sent piecemeal or one requirement at a time stand a much higher chance of becoming lost in the mails, misplaced when they are received, or separated into different folders, especially if there is a change in the person filling the office of Preceptor. We cannot review your work until the entire set of requirements is received. If you would like to check your work, you have a few options, including posting your work to ADF-Dedicants or asking one of the Mentors or Deputy Preceptors to look over your work.

You may also send it (copies **only**, no originals, and only if you have no means of submitting it electronically) to:

ADF
C/O ADF Preceptor
P.O. Box 17874
Tucson, AZ 85731-7874

But please only send it via mail if you cannot upload a digital copy.

The ADF Preceptor will assign a reviewer for your work and let you know if it is satisfactory. If you have worked through this full year and taken the notes required, you shouldn't have any problems. If something stands out to the Preceptor as either incomplete or not quite up to snuff, she or he will return it to you and request that you re-work it. You will also receive suggestions on how to fix it.

A Particularly Important Note:

When you submit your work, it is entirely possible that you'll find it rejected by your reviewer: don't lose heart! This is a normal (and even *expected*) part of the review process. Very often, even the best, most well-versed ADF members will have something in a submission that's not clear, doesn't quite fit the requirement, or isn't exactly as spot-on as you might like.

And that's okay. It's worth saying that I had virtually every one of my study program courses rejected on submission, occasionally more than once, to make sure that they were "up to snuff." It's never about a reviewer disliking you, or wanting to push you harder than they push others.

The Path Ahead

Now, it's up to you to decide where to go. The documentation for this Path is over, but the journey has just begun. You've worked very hard, and you should be very proud of yourself. The next steps may include moving onto a study program, looking into clergy training, mentoring other Dedicants, or perhaps all of the above.

Again, congratulations, and thank you for being such a valuable part of the vision of ADF!

Bright Blessings!
-Rev. Michael J Dangler

Appendix 1: Resources and Rituals for the Wheel of the Year

Each of these resource lists are designed to help you think about the eight ADF High Days and write rituals for each, especially if you're solitary.

Resources on the Wheel of the Year in General

- "Pagan Piety: Keeping the Old Ways" by Ian Corrigan, in the *DP Handbook* and at <http://www.adf.org/training/piety.html>;
- The "Liturgy and Rituals" section of the ADF site, <http://www.adf.org/rituals/index.html>;
- "Essay on Pagan Piety" by Melissa Jenkins, <http://www.adf.org/members/training/dp/examples/melissa-jenkins/piety.html>;
- "Essay on Pagan Piety" by Shawn Miller, <http://www.adf.org/members/training/dp/examples/shawn-miller/piety.html>;
- "The Norse Wheel of the Year" by Paul Maurice, <http://www.adf.org/articles/cosmology/norsewy.html>;
- *The Wheel of the Year at Muin Mound Grove, ADF: A Cycle of Druid Rituals* by Rev. Skip Ellison
- *Sunna's Journey: Norse Liturgy Through the Wheel of the Year* by Nicholas Egelhoff

Resources on Ritual in General

- Three Cranes Grove, ADF's, *The Fire on Our Hearth – A Three Cranes Devotional*,
  Available through <http://www.cafepress.com/3cgshop>
- The "Liturgy and Rituals" section of the ADF site, <http://www.adf.org/rituals/index.html>;
- The "Explanations of ADF Ritual" section of the ADF site, <http://www.adf.org/rituals/explanations/>;
- "The COoR as Mexican Burrito" by Rev. Michael J Dangler <http://www.adf.org/members/training/dp/articles/mexican-burrito.html>
- "Chants and Songs" <http://www.adf.org/rituals/chants/>;
- "Meditations" <http://www.adf.org/rituals/meditations/>

Samhain Resources

"Background on Samhain" by Ian Corrigan, <http://www.adf.org/rituals/celtic/samhain/background.html>;
"Samhain Lore" by Ian Corrigan, <http://www.adf.org/rituals/celtic/samhain/scg-samhain-

99-lore.html>;
"Raven" by Jessica Sanchez, <http://www.adf.org/articles/gods-and-spirits/nature/raven.html>;
The Solitary Druid by Rev. Skip Ellison, p. 92-99

Samhain Ritual Resources

The "Samhain Ritual" pages at <http://www.adf.org/rituals/celtic/samhain/>;
Sacred Fire, Holy Well by Ian Corrigan, p. 118-123;
The Solitary Druid by Rev. Skip Ellison, p. 99-112
The Fire on Our Hearth by Three Cranes Grove, ADF, p. 110-115

Winter Solstice Resources

"The Old Man at the Year's End" by Errach of Pittsburgh,
<http://www.adf.org/rituals/celtic/yule/old-man-at-years-end.html>;
The Solitary Druid by Rev. Skip Ellison, p. 155-158

Winter Solstice Ritual Resources

"Winter Solstice" by Amergin Aryson,
<http://www.adf.org/rituals/celtic/yule/wsolstice.html>;
"A Solitary Yule" by Rev. Michael J Dangler, <http://www.adf.org/rituals/celtic/yule/sol-yule-mjd.html>;
The Fire on Our Hearth by Three Cranes Grove, ADF, p. 115-122
The Solitary Druid by Rev. Skip Ellison, p. 159-169

Imbolc Resources

"Imbolc Traditions" by Fox, <http://www.adf.org/rituals/celtic/imbolc/imbolc-traditions.html>;
"Imbolc" section, <http://www.threecranes.org/hhd/#imbolc>;
The Solitary Druid by Rev. Skip Ellison, p. 112-117

Imbolc Ritual Resources

"Sonoran Sunrise Grove Imbolc 2004", <http://www.adf.org/rituals/celtic/imbolc/ssg-imbolc-04.html>;
"Disting" by Paul Maurice, <http://www.adf.org/rituals/norse/disting/disting.html>;
Sacred Fire, Holy Well by Ian Corrigan, p. 124-127;
The Solitary Druid by Rev. Skip Ellison, p. 117-128

Spring Equinox Resources

"Just What is Equinox" by Errach of Pittsburgh,
<http://www.adf.org/rituals/explanations/what-is-an-equinox.html>;
The Solitary Druid by Rev. Skip Ellison, p. 169-171

Spring Equinox Ritual Resources

"Nemos Ognios Spring Equinox, 2005" by Ceisiwr Serith,
<http://www.adf.org/rituals/proto-indo-european/ostara.html>:
"Gleichennacht" by Paul Maurice,
<http://www.adf.org/rituals/norse/gleichennacht/gleichennacht.html>;
"Solitary Spring Equinox Rite" by Amanda Lynne Orcutt,
<http://www.adf.org/rituals/hellenic/sp-eq-solitary.html>
The Solitary Druid by Rev. Skip Ellison, p. 171-176
The Fire on Our Hearth by Three Cranes Grove, ADF, p. 122-126

Beltaine Resources

"On Beltane" by Errach of Pittsburgh, <http://www.adf.org/rituals/celtic/beltainne/on-beltane.html>;
The Solitary Druid by Rev. Skip Ellison, p. 128-136

Beltaine Ritual Resources

"Beltane" by Ceisiwr Serith, <http://www.adf.org/rituals/celtic/beltainne/cei-beltane.html>;
"Beltainne Rite" by Ian Corrigan,
<http://www.adf.org/rituals/celtic/beltainne/beltainne.html>;
"Maitag" by Paul Maurice, <http://www.adf.org/rituals/norse/maitag/maitag.html>;
Sacred Fire, Holy Well by Ian Corrigan, p. 128-133;
The Solitary Druid by Rev. Skip Ellison, p. 136-145

Summer Solstice Resources

"What Would the Druids Do at the Summer Solstice?" by Errach of Pittsburgh,
<http://www.adf.org/rituals/celtic/midsummer/wwtdd-summer-solstice.html>;
The Solitary Druid by Rev. Skip Ellison, p. 176-180

Summer Solstice Ritual Resources

"Sonoran Sunrise Grove Midsummer Ritual"
<http://www.adf.org/rituals/celtic/midsummer/ssgmidsummer.html>;
The Solitary Druid by Rev. Skip Ellison, p. 180-186

Lughnassadh Resources

"On Lughnassadh" by Ian Corrigan, <http://www.adf.org/rituals/celtic/lughnassadh/on-lughnassadh.html>;
"On the Nature of Sovereignty" by Errach of Pittsburgh,
<http://www.adf.org/rituals/celtic/lughnassadh/nature-of-sovereignty.html>;
The Solitary Druid by Rev. Skip Ellison, p. 145-149

Lughnassadh Ritual Resources

"A Celtic Lughnasad Module" by Ceisiwr Serith,
<http://www.adf.org/rituals/celtic/lughnassadh/cei-lughnasad.html>;
Sacred Fire, Holy Well by Ian Corrigan, p. 134-137;
The Solitary Druid by Rev. Skip Ellison, p. 149-154

Autumn Equinox Resources

"Just What is Equinox" by Rev. Errach of Pittsburgh,
<http://www.adf.org/rituals/explanations/what-is-an-equinox.html>;
"Autumnal Equinox" section, <http://www.threecranes.org/hhd/#auequinox>;
The Solitary Druid by Rev. Skip Ellison, p. 187-189

Autumn Equinox Ritual Resources

"Gleichentag Rituals" <http://www.adf.org/rituals/norse/gleichentag/>;
The Solitary Druid by Rev. Skip Ellison, p. 189-195

Appendix 2: Ritual Write-up Template

We have provided a template that you can expand on for writing up rituals. Feel free to re-write it, edit it, or make copies of it. The template here is derived from Sonoran Sunrise Grove, ADF's, Ritual Service Record. Special thanks to Rev. Kirk Thomas for providing it.

High Day Celebrated: _____   **Location:** _____

Date Celebrated: _____   **Time Celebrated:** _____

Who Led the Rite: _____   **Grove Name:** _____

Other ritual officers: _____

Number of Attendees: _____   **Gatekeeper:** _____

Deities of the Occasion (Patrons): _____

Omen Method (i.e. runes, ogham, tarot): _____

Omen (as read, with interpretation):

_____
_____
_____
_____
_____
_____
_____
_____

Any Magical Workings Done or Oaths Given:

_____
_____
_____

Impressions/Other Comments/Notes:

_____
_____
_____
_____
_____

Appendix 3: Citations for Your Work

Citations in a certain style have never been required as part of the DP; it was always enough to provide a clear indication of where you got the information. Still, a good citation is the best way to do this, so we'll provide citations that you can use for the most common material cited in this work.

The aim is to make it easy on you: you should just be able to copy/paste these into your Works Cited page (check the info first, though, as new editions of books might have different publishers or years; also, replace "[date accessed]" with today's date on any electronic items below):

Our Own Druidry (2009 Ed.)
- Physical Book:
  - Corrigan, Ian. *Our Own Druidry: An Introduction to Ár nDraíocht Féin and the Druid Path.* Tucson, AZ: ADF Publishing, 2009. Print.
- PDF from the ADF website:
  - Corrigan, Ian. *Our Own Druidry: An Introduction to Ár nDraíocht Féin and the Druid Path.* Ár nDraíocht Féin, 2009. PDF file. [date accessed].

The ADF Membership Guide (5th Ed)
- Physical Book:
  - Ár nDraíocht Féin. *ADF Membership Guide, Fifth Edition.* Tucson, AZ: ADF Publishing, 2009. Print.
- PDF from the ADF website:
  - Ár nDraíocht Féin. *ADF Membership Guide, Fifth Edition.* Ár nDraíocht Féin, 2009. PDF file. [date accessed].

The DP WotY (this book)
- Physical Book:
  - Dangler, Michael J. *The ADF Dedicant Path Through the Wheel of the Year.* Columbus, OH: Garanus Publishing, 2016. Print.
- PDF from the ADF website:
  - Dangler, Michael J. *The ADF Dedicant Path Through the Wheel of the Year.* Ár nDraíocht Féin, 2016. PDF file. [date accessed].

Skip's *Solitary Druid*
- Ellison, Robert Lee (Skip). *The Solitary Druid: Walking the Path of Wisdom and Spirit.* Tucson, AZ: ADF Publishing, 2013. Print.

Ian's *Sacred Fire, Holy Well*
- Corrigan, Ian. *Sacred Fire, Holy Well: A Druid's Companion.* Tucson, AZ: ADF Publishing, 2006. Print.

Cei's *A Book of Pagan Prayer*
- Serith, Ceisiwr. *A Book of Pagan Prayer*. Tucson, AZ: Weiser Books, 2002. Print.

Nick's *Sunna's Journey*
- Egelhoff, Nicholas. *Sunna's Journey: Norse Liturgy Through the Wheel of the Year*. Columbus, OH: Garanus Publishing, 2013. Print.

Kirk's *Sacred Gifts*
- Thomas, Kirk S. *Sacred Gifts: Reciprocity and the Gods*. Tucson, AZ: ADF Publishing, 2015. Print.

MJD's *A Breviary for Cranes, Solitary*
- Physical Book:
  - Dangler, Michael. *A Crane Breviary and Guide Book: Rituals For the Cranes of ADF, When They Must Kindle Their Own Good Fire*. Columbus, OH: Garanus Publishing, 2010. Print.
- PDF from the ADF website:
  - Dangler, Michael. *A Crane Breviary and Guide Book: Rituals For the Cranes of ADF, When They Must Kindle Their Own Good Fire*. Ár nDraíocht Féin, 2010. PDF file. [date accessed]

Appendix 4: Rune, Ogham, and Greek Quick Reference Charts

Table A: Runes

Rune	Name	Translation(s); Meaning(s)
ᚠ	Fehu	**Cattle;** movable wealth, generosity
ᚢ	Uruz	**Auroch, drizzle;** strength, dross
ᚦ	Þurisaz	**Giant, thorn;** chaotic, brute strength
ᚨ	Ansuz	**Mouth, god;** beginnings, communication
ᚱ	Raiðo	**Journey;** horse-and-rider, partnership
ᚲ	Kenaz	**Torch, ulcer;** cheer, pain, death
ᚷ	Gebo	**Gift;** reciprocity, **ghos-ti-*
ᚹ	Wunjo	**Joy;** bliss
ᚺ	Hagalaz	**Hail;** destruction, challenge
ᚾ	Nauðiz	**Need;** oppression, lessons learned
ᛁ	Isa	**Ice;** beautiful and dangerous
ᛃ	Jera	**Year;** good harvest, hard work
ᛇ	Eihwaz	**Yew;** ancient lore, helping and hurting
ᛈ	Perþo	**Dice cup, vulva;** joy, uncertainty
ᛉ	Algiz	**Elk-sedge;** offensive/defensive balance
ᛋ	Sowilo	**Sun;** warmth, strength, promise, cycles
ᛏ	Tiwaz	**Tir;** guidance, justice, navigation
ᛒ	Berkano	**Birch;** strength, flexibility, resourcefulness
ᛖ	Ehwaz	**Horse;** easy and joyful travel, help
ᛗ	Mannaz	**Man;** self, mortality, *orlog*, kinship
ᛚ	Laguz	**Water;** change, hidden wealth, flowing
ᛜ	Ingwaz	**Ing;** fertility, ancestors
ᛞ	Dagaz	**Day;** rising sun, new day, deliverance
ᛟ	Oþila	**Enclosure;** stationary wealth, ancestors, completion

TIP 1: If you do not own your own symbol set, you can draw the symbols on index cards for a quick, makeshift rune or ogham deck. Alternatively, you can purchase some craft wood at your local craft store and draw the symbols on with a permanent marker.

TIP 2: On ogham tiles, put a small inverted "v" on the bottom of the line that runs down the middle. Having the ^ at the bottom of the few will help you determine which end is "up." Runes are unique enough not to require directional assistance.

Table B: Ogham

Few	Name	Tree	Meaning(s)
⊢	Beith	**Birch**	New beginnings, purification
⊨	Luis	**Rowan**	Beauty and delight, magical protection
⊫	Fern	**Alder**	Protection, guidance
	Sail	**Willow**	Liminality, flow
	Nion	**Ash**	Weaver's beam, connection
⊣	Uath	**Hawthorn**	Fear, despair, cleansing
	Dair	**Oak**	Strength, knowledge
	Tinne	**Holly**	Balance, mastery
	Coll	**Hazel**	Wisdom
	Ceirt	**Apple**	The Otherworld, shelter, choice
	Muin	**Vine**	Challenge, communication, inspiration
	Gort	**Ivy**	Growth, pathways
	nGéadal	**Broom**	Healing and tools
	Straif	**Blackthorn**	Secrets, strife, transformation
	Ruis	**Elder**	Passion, embarrassment, endings
	Ailm	**Silver Fir**	Foresight, inception, perspective
	Onn	**Gorse**	Easy travel, wheel, movement
	Úr	**Heather**	Earth and growth, death
	Eadhadh	**Aspen**	Grief and fear, vision, communication
	Iodhadh	**Yew**	Ancestors and death, memory
✕	Éabhadh	**Poplar**	Buoyancy and healing, rising up
◇	Ór	**Spindle**	Work, building, wealth, domesticity
	Uillean	**Honeysuckle**	Drawing together, sweetness
	Phagos	**Beech**	Ancestral knowledge
	Emancholl	**Witchhazel**	Magic, illness/healing

Table C: Greek Alphabet Oracle

Letter	Name	Number	Keyword & Meaning(s)
Α	Alpha	30-30; 1	*Hapanta* – Everything
Β	Beta	29-28; 2	*Boêthos* – Assistant
Γ	Gamma	28-27; 3	*Gê* – Gaia [Earth]
Δ	Delta	27-26; 4	*Dunamis* – Strength
Ε	Epsilon	26-25; 5	*Erôs* – Desire
Ι	Zeta	24-24; 7	*Zalê* – Storm
Η	Eta	23-23; 8	*Hêlios* – Helios [Sun]
Θ	Theta	22-22; 9	*Theoi* – Gods
Ι	Iota	21-21; 10	*Hidrôs* – Sweat
Κ	Kappa	20-20; 20	*Kuma* – Waves
Λ	Lambda	19-19; 30	*Laios* – Left
Μ	Mu	18-18; 40	*Mokhthos* – Labor
Ν	Nu	17-17; 50	*Neikêphoros* - Strife
Ξ	Xi	16-16; 60	*Xêros* - Withered
Ο	Omicron	15-15; 70	*Ouk esti* - There is Not
Π	Pi	14-14; 80	*Polla* - Many
Ρ	Rho	12-13; 100	*Rhaion* - Easily
Σ	Sigma	12-12; 200	*Saphôs* - Plainly
Τ	Tau	10-11; 300	*Tôn Parousôn* - From the Companions
Υ	Upsilon	9-10; 400	*Huposkhesis* - Undertaking
Φ	Phi	8-9; 500	*Phaulos* - Carelessly
Χ	Khi	7-8; 600	*Khruseos* - Golden
Ψ	Psi	6-7; 700	*Psêphos* - Judgement
Ω	Omega	5-5; 800	*Ômos* - Difficult

Note on Letters: Letters displayed are archaic Greek letters, not modern
Note on Numbers: The first number is for casting 5 dice, the second for casting 5 *astragaloi* (sheep knuckelbones), and the third number is the traditional number associated with that Greek letter.
More info at https://web.eecs.utk.edu/~mclennan/BA/GAO.html

Made in United States
Orlando, FL
04 March 2023

30592940R00076